Language Matters

BOOK D

Graham Ryles

Rod Campbell

Judy Coghill

OXFORD

UNIVERSITY PRESS

OXFORD
UNIVERSITY PRESS

70 Wynford Drive, Don Mills, Ontario M3C 1J9
www.oup.com/ca

Oxford University Press is a department of the University of Oxford.
It furthers the University's objective of excellence in research, scholarship,
and education by publishing worldwide in

Oxford New York

Auckland Bangkok Buenos Aires Cape Town Chennai
Dar es Salaam Delhi Hong Kong Istanbul Karachi Kolkata
Kuala Lumpur Madrid Melbourne Mexico City Mumbai Nairobi
São Paulo Shanghai Taipei Tokyo Toronto

Oxford is a trade mark of Oxford University Press
in the UK and in certain other countries

Published in Canada
by Oxford University Press

This book was adapted from material originally published by Oxford University Press, Australia.

Library and Archives Canada Cataloguing in Publication

Ryles, Graham

　　Language matters : book D / Graham Ryles, Rod Campbell, Judy Coghill.

ISBN 0-19-542157-4

　　1. English language—Composition and exercises—Juvenile literature. 2. English language—Problems, exercises,
etc.—Juvenile literature. I. Campbell, Rod II. Coghill, Judith Ann, 1948- III. Title.

LB1576.R945 2004　　　　　428.2　　　　　C2004-904413-3

Cover Design: Brett Miller
Cover Illustration: Carl Wiens
Edited by Sally Green
Internal illustrations: Celina Mosbauer, Melissa Smith
Typeset: Sandra Sheehan

This book is printed on permanent (acid-free) paper ∞.
Printed in Canada

1 2 3 4　　04 05 06 07

Contents

General overview

Book D	Text	Grammar	Sentence construction	Punctuation
Narrative	*Joan of Arc*, p. viii	Noun–pronoun agreement Adjectives: comparative and superlative degree		Titles: Capital letters
	Excalibur, p. 30	Noun–pronoun agreement Verbs: am, is, are, was, were Adverbs: comparative degree		Commas
	Scott of the Antarctic, p. 60	Incomplete clauses Adjectives	Adjectives: comparative, superlative	Commas with clauses
	Leiningen versus the ants, p. 90	Subject–verb agreement	Verbs and adjectives	Commas
Transaction	Greetings, p. 4	Subject groups	Subject–verb agreement	Semi-colon
	Questionnaires, p. 34	Subject groups	Sentence fragments	
	Meeting agendas, p. 64	Subject groups		Agendas (layout)
	Speeches: Introducing a guest speaker, p. 94	Subordinate clauses	Loose and periodic sentences	
Explanation	Rest and sleep are good for you, p. 8	Tense: past and present		Abbreviations
	Reading bus timetables, p. 38	Could have	Clause completion	Colons in lists
	Magnets, p. 68	Infinitive form Split infinitives Verb forms		
	What makes an electric bell ring?, p. 98	Relative clauses	Pronouns and their references	Hyphens

General overview

Book D	Text	Grammar	Sentence construction	Punctuation
Report	Halley's Comet, p. 12	Relative clauses and relative pronouns	Constructing meaning in context	Verbs written as numerals
	A close encounter with nature, p. 42	Theme and rheme	Constructing meaning in context	
	Watching in anticipation, p. 72	Incomplete clauses Sentence completion		Hyphens
	Film reviews, p. 102	Loose and periodic sentences	Constructing meaning in context	Colon
Procedure	Map reading: China, p. 16	Past tense	Dangling participle	Colon and commas with lists
	High jump: scissors style, p. 46	Voice: active/passive	Tenses: past, present	
	Assembling a scooter, p. 76	Imperative mood	Dangling participle	Brackets Bullets
	Science experiment, p. 106	Participles and gerunds	Tenses: past and future	
Letter writing	Informal notes, p. 20	Tense: infinitive, past, simple present participle, past participle		Period Abbreviations
	Formal party invitation, p. 50	each, every, etc. take singular verb		
	Letters seeking and giving information, p. 80	Subject–verb agreement		Period Question mark Exclamation mark
	Letters of complaint and praise, p. 110	Subject–verb agreement		

To the teacher

Language Matters is a sequentially developed series of six books, designed to reflect the notion of activities "in context." This series is designed to support, structure, reinforce and/or extend your writing program throughout a school year. At the end of each term, there is a series of summative writing activities. Because the students are given many opportunities during the term to learn different forms of writing and to practise key writing skills, the results of the end of term assessments provide you and the student with clear indicators of writing strengths and areas requiring further work.

The activities in this workbook can be assigned to individual students, students working in small groups or in pairs, or to the class as a whole. You then have opportunities to work with individuals or small groups of students, as needed. This series is also flexible in that if a student needs more work in a certain area, you can direct them to specific exercises in a previous book. Similarly, for students in need of more challenge, you can direct them to exercises in the next book in the series.

In addition, this series uses readings related to other subject areas. As a result, it provides models for different types of writing (e.g., letters, reports, ads, stories, interviews) and stresses the importance of literacy in many different subjects. The skills and knowledge that are taught in this series support the learning expectations in your language arts curriculum related to

- grammar
- punctuation
- sentences
- paragraphs
- spelling
- vocabulary building.

Also, several units focus on required skills of visual presentation.

Each unit gives students the opportunity to gain the skills and knowledge they will need to become fine writers. To reinforce this new learning, the "Over to you" section at the end of each unit requires students to practise and apply their skills in open-ended short and long writing pieces.

To the student

Hello and welcome,

This workbook will help you develop and grow as a writer. Each unit begins with a different kind of writing such as poetry, letters, stories, and reports, for example. In each unit of work, you will learn important writing skills and you will learn more about words, sentences, paragraphs, grammar, spelling and punctuation. In the "Over to you" section at the end of each unit, you will be able to apply your new learning about writing in creative and different ways.

At the end of each term, it's important to reflect on what you have learned about writing and what you need to continue to work at. At the end of each term, there is a series of summative writing activities. Returning to the results of these activities before you start each new term will help remind you of what you have accomplished and what you will be working to improve in your writing.

Being a good writer—a clear and easy communicator—is very helpful in school, in work and in all parts of life. So, turn the page and let's get started!

Joan of Arc

Read the text and answer the questions.

Jeanne d'Arc (1412–31) is a French national hero and saint. She is also known as the Maid of Orleans. She was the daughter of a farmer and grew up in the French province of Lorraine. She began to hear voices, which urged her to leave home and to help Charles, the heir to the French throne, to become crowned as King of France.

The English King was at war with the French King, and so Joan knew she was being asked by her voices to fight the English. She was 16 when she left home to meet Charles. She dressed as a young man, and although everyone laughed at her, she convinced Charles that she could help him.

Charles gave her soldiers and a general. Joan was not a military leader but she gave the French soldiers a fighting spirit and morale. In May 1429, she forced the enemy to give up their siege at Orleans and later defeated the English at Patay.

Because of Joan's inspired victories, Charles could be crowned King of France at Rheims. She was with him, and she had reached the pinnacle of her fortunes. She felt that she had done her duty and could go home. However, she agreed to fight on.

Later in 1429 she was captured by the Burgundians at the siege of Paris and sold to their English allies. The English judges tried her as a witch, saying that her voices came from the devil. She was kept in prison for more than a year before the English judges, all churchmen, found her guilty and she was burned to death at Rouen.

King Charles of France never made any attempt to rescue her, but in 1456 he recognized the value of her service to France. The French were inspired in their new war against the English when they remembered what she had done for them.

Joan's short life and outstanding actions became the base for many legends. She appears in the literature, theatre and music of many European countries, and in 1920 she was canonized as a saint of the Catholic Church.

It is more than 570 years since her terrible death, but Joan of Arc is regarded by many people as one of the greatest women who ever lived.

1   In what year was Joan of Arc put to death? _____

2   What is the French name for Joan? _____

3 Name four French cities that feature in her story. _____

_____

4 Joan heard voices talking only to her. What did these voices tell her to do?

_____

_____

5 What did the English judges think about Joan and her voices?

_____

_____

6 How can anyone be a military success yet have no knowledge of military leadership? Discuss your answer with a student in your class and your teacher.

Grammar

Noun–pronoun agreement

Choose from the pronouns in brackets to complete the sentences.

1 Joan left _____ home to help Charles and _____ convinced

_____ of _____ mission. (he, she, her, his, him, hers)

2 The King provided _____ with some of _____ troops. (she, her, him, his)

3 The French soldiers became very loyal to _____ inspirational young leader. (her, they, she's, their)

4 The Duke of Burgundy captured _____ and sold _____ to the English. (her, she, hers)

5 _____ is a story of triumph and tragedy. (she, her, hers, she's)

Adjectives: comparative and superlative degree

The comparative degree of the adjective is used when comparing two things.
Example This car is **faster** than that car.
The superlative degree is used when there are more than two things compared.
Example This is the **fastest** car in the world.

Complete the sentences by using the correct form of the adjective in the brackets.

1   Joan of Arc soon showed that she was among the _____ of the French leaders. (brave)

2   Joan of Arc was not a soldier, but she proved to be a _____ leader than many of the military leaders. (good)

3   Joan of Arc is probably the _____ known woman in Western history. (good)

4   The English soldiers and judges were _____ once Joan was in their prison. (happy)

Punctuation

Proper names of people and places, as well as their titles and the titles of books, films and plays, begin with a capital letter.
Example Mary, London, Montreal, King Henry, Governor General, Mayor Bill Smith, *The Sound of Music*.
These capital letters are kept no matter where the words appear in a sentence or in a quotation.

Circle the errors in the use of capital letters.

"I don't know about joan," said andrew Lloyd-Webber as he considered

the question from the reporter. "I would like to write a musical about her

but there have been so many plays and films about her. george bernard

shaw wrote the best play, I think, and I would use it as a basis for a

musical called jeanne. The big problem is finding a title for a love song,

such as 'my love' or 'a soldier's dream'."

Word knowledge

SPELL CHECK

Learn these words. Look, say, cover, write and check. Repeat until the word is spelled correctly.

disgraceful	dismiss	distress	discover
display	disturbing	disgusted	disobey
disappeared	disappointed	disadvantaged	disgrace

1 Write the words in your spelling list and test yourself.
2 Write the words in sentences.

Write the correct form of the words in brackets.

1 The _____ (disgrace) behaviour of the students was

_____ (discover) by the principal.

2 The cat _____ (disappear) down the hole.

3 The man _____ (disobey) the traffic light.

4 I was _____ (distress) that you were _____
(disappoint) with the result.

Over to you "Writing Process"

When you are assigned a piece of writing, you should always use the process outlined below. Following these steps will make your work the best writing it can be.
1 Write the first draft.
2 Ask a classmate to read the draft and make suggestions for improvement in
   • Ordering the sentences and ideas
   • Focussing on one thing
   • Adding interesting details
3 Revise your first draft using the suggestions of your classmate. Proofread your work for
   • Spelling
   • Grammar
   • Sentence structure
   • Word use
4 Ask a friend to check your draft for all the same things.
5 Then, neatly write your final copy.

Greetings

Read the text and answer the questions.

Greeting other people is the first and most important social event in our lives. Parents greet their children as soon as they are born, and it is not long before babies know who is who among the people in their everyday lives.

After only a few months, babies work out systems of greetings for meeting people they know and those people who are unfamiliar. Have you ever seen a four-month-old baby staring at you? Have you smiled and said "hello" to the baby? Then have you watched the baby's little frown as it realizes that it does not know you? Either the baby will begin to make strange noises and cling to its caregiver, or it will jerk its head in such a way that its whole body moves, and smile at you.

The baby has learned to greet people and to respond to greetings at a very early age. What it has learned is the most important aspect of a greeting: the facial and body gestures that accompany the smile. These are signals that indicate friendliness.

Secondly, there is the intonation in the voice. Greetings are said warmly, with an expression anywhere between bright quickness and easy-going friendliness.

The third aspect concerns the words chosen. Together, the words, their intonation and the facial expression signal a greeting. These indicators are the same all over the world.

There may be a little difference in the words used, but "Good day," "Bongiorno," "Nihao," "Bonjour" and "Guten Morgen" all contain the word "good." The common greeting from other languages is translated into English as "Good Day" or "Hello." "Konnichi-wa" means "good day."

There are thousands of languages and cultures around the world, but though the words are different, they mean the same. And they are accompanied with friendly gestures, with smiles and with pleasant vocal intonation. You learned all of these skills easily and naturally in the first months and years of your life.

1   What is the most important indicator of a greeting?

_____

2   When do most people learn these signals?

_____

3 How do babies learn that someone is friendly?

_____

4 What are the three indicators of a greeting?

_____

5 What would you think if any one of these indicators was missing from a greeting?

_____

6 What do "bon," "hao" and "guten" mean?

_____

Grammar

Subject groups

A subject group is a group of words that functions together with the main noun before or after the verb. A subject group may be one word or many words in length. The subject groups in the following sentences are underlined.

<u>Cards</u> can be sent anywhere.

<u>Greeting cards</u> can be sent anywhere.

<u>Birthday cards that carry great messages for your friends</u> can be sent anywhere.

The main noun, head noun or subject in each sentence is "cards." Any other words added to "cards" tell more about "cards," and belong in that group. The underlined groups are known as subject groups.

1 Underline the subject groups before the verb phrase "makes for." The main noun or subject is "smile."

   a) A smile makes for friendly greeting.

   b) A smile with kind words makes for a friendly greeting.

   c) A smile that comes with a kind word and a pleasant voice makes for the friendliest greeting.

   d) A warm smile that accompanies a pleasantly spoken and kind word makes for a greeting that will be remembered.

2 Read the sentences above and circle the subject groups after the verb phrase. The main noun is "greeting."

Sentence construction

There are problems with agreement between the subject and the verb in the sentences below. Rewrite the sentences correctly.

1 Getting birthday cards are good presents, especially if they contain money.

   _____

   _____

2 Once upon a time there were an old man who would not send birthday cards to his friends.

   _____

   _____

3 Because Jane and Serena is too young, their mothers writes their greetings on the cards for them.

   _____

   _____

4 When two people greet each other in two different languages, a problem occurs if there is no warmth to their words and faces.

   _____

   _____

5 When two people hold a conversation in different languages, there is problems in communication.

   _____

   _____

Word knowledge

SPELL CHECK

Learn these words. Look, say, cover, write and check. Repeat until the word is spelled correctly.

successful   succeed   occurred   occupied   barrier   carrier
carriage   marriage   hurriedly   hurricane   terrified   terrific

1 Write the words in your spelling list and test yourself.
2 Write the words in sentences.

Write the correct form of the words in brackets.

1 Hurricane-force winds _____ (occur) along the coast,

    _____ (force) the _____ (terrify) population to leave

    _____ (hurry).

2 The strikers _____ (occupy) the gateway, _____ (prevent)

    _____ (carriage) from _____ (enter) the terminal.

3 Many soccer fans _____ (succeed) in _____ (occupy) the
    front seats two hours ago.

Over to you

1 Survey the children in your school to find out how many speak a language other than English. Ask those children how they greet each other in their own language. Make a chart of the numbers of different greetings that can be given by the children in your school.
2 Make charts of greetings for New Year and Happy Birthday, using as many different languages as you can find.

Rest and sleep are good for you

1   Read the text and answer the questions.

Have you ever asked why you need to sleep?

All children have asked their parents why they should go to bed early, but few people question the need to sleep. Sleep is necessary for health and well-being. While you are sleeping, your body and its internal organs do not have to work as hard as when you are awake and active. Your body rests, and you wake up ready to begin a new day fresh and alert.

What happens to you when you are sleeping?

While you are sleeping, many changes take place in your body. For most of the time, your heartbeat and breathing rate slow down. Muscle and nerve tissues repair themselves, and nutrients from your evening meal are digested and stored for use when you wake up.

   Your brain quietly and automatically regulates the activities of your body; and in your mind, you go over the events and problems of the previous day. Did you realize that sleeping helps you to relax, helps you to see problems differently and to think of better solutions to problems?

What happens if you do not have enough sleep?

People who do not have enough sleep are always tired, and not able to work, learn and enjoy life as well as they could. People who do not get enough sleep over a long period of time will become ill, and may suffer physical and psychological problems. In fact, missing out on sleep would make your biography a short one.

a) What happens when you go to sleep?

_____

_____

b) Why would a good sleep make the following day less stressful?

_____

_____

c) What parts of your body repair themselves while you are resting?

_____

d) Complete the passage.

Sleep is necessary for _____ and _____ . While you

are _____ , your _____ and its _____

do not _____ to _____ as _____ as

when you are _____ and _____ .

Grammar

The past tense

> An explanation, description or report of an event is often written in the past tense. Note the use of the verbs in the past tense in the text below.
>
> Yesterday, the winter sun shone brightly and our family decided to go to the Whispering Pines Park for a picnic. It was cold under the trees, so we wore sunscreen and hats and played in the sun. It was not long before we had to take off our sweaters. The activity sharpened our appetite, and we ate a big picnic lunch that our parents prepared. After lunch, we packed the plates and put the garbage in the cans at the park. Then we went for a walk in the woods as the afternoon sunlight angled through the trees.

1   Make a list of the verbs in the past tense used in the text above. There are 14 of them, and they are the processes that are so important in each sentence. Try reading the paragraph without these verbs.

_____   _____

_____   _____

_____   _____

_____   _____

_____   _____

_____   _____

_____   _____

2 However, there are times when only the present tense can be used, particularly when you write about something that exists. Rewrite the following story by changing the tense of the verbs from present to past tense. There are two verbs that must remain in the present tense. Underline these two verbs.

> The trip is long and very tiring, but it is worth the effort. The bus bounces from one pothole in the terrible road to the next, but the scenery is spectacular. We really appreciate it when the driver stops to let us see the beautiful scenery and take photographs. The lighthouse stands forever like a guard for the harbour and the people who live nearby.

_____

_____

_____

_____

_____

_____

Punctuation

Abbreviations often use the first and last letters of the word, followed by a period (e.g. Missus = Mrs.). Days and months have their own abbreviations (e.g., February = Feb., Saturday = Sat.) and are followed by periods.

Write the abbreviations for these words.

1 Street _____   4 Tuesday _____   7 Avenue _____

2 Mister _____   5 October _____   8 Centimetre _____

3 January _____   6 Doctor _____   9 September _____

Word knowledge

SPELL CHECK

Learn these words. Look, say, cover, write and check. Repeat until the word is spelled correctly.

label	panel	travelling	collapsed	excellent	consent
current	recent	innocently	continent	violently	event

1 Write the words in your spelling list and test yourself.
2 Write the words in sentences.

Word forms

Write the correct form of the words in brackets.

1 The gorilla was in a _____ (travel) circus, which

_____ (recent) visited our town.

2 My umbrella _____ (collapse) in the heavy rain, which

_____ (violent) lashed the _____ (event) at our

local show.

3 The parcel was _____ (label), _____ (address) and

_____ (dispatch) for _____ (mail).

Over to you

1 What do you know about REMs? When do these appear as you sleep? What do the researchers think is happening during REM sleep?
2 Caffeine and a number of other substances can keep people awake for long periods of time. Can these substances be used as a substitute for sleep? Why? Why not?

Explanation: Rest and sleep are good for you   **11**

Halley's Comet

Read the report and match the information.

Comets are bright objects that are seen in the night sky. What can be seen is the tail, which is made up of gas and dust particles. Most comets orbit the sun.

People long ago thought that seeing a comet meant disaster or unhappy events. Comets were believed to be omens of doom for the Saxons in CE 1066.

Sightings of comets have been recorded in 240 BCE, in CE 1066 and at other times, but it was not until 1705 that the return of one was predicted. Edmund Halley (1656–1742), an English astronomer and mathematician, said that the comet seen in 1682 was the same as the one last seen in 1607 and 1531. He predicted that the comet would return in late 1758 or early 1759.

The comet returned in 1759. Since then it has returned in 1835, 1910 and 1986. Its orbital period is about 76 years. It is named after Edmund Halley.

Match the information in the left-hand column with the information in the right-hand column.

1	Comets	a	Edmund Halley
2	Comet tail	b	gas and dust
3	240 BCE	c	omens of doom or signs of change
4	CE 2062	d	first reported sighting of Halley's Comet
5	CE 1682	e	first reported sighting of a comet
6	Astronomer	f	next sighting of Halley's Comet
7	CE 1066	g	report of a comet as omen for battle

Grammar

Relative clauses and relative pronouns

The most common relative pronouns are **who**, **which**, **whom**, **whose** and **that**.

1   Circle the relative pronoun in each sentence.
Example Comets are bright objects (which) are seen in the night sky.

a)   Comets were thought to be omens that signified momentous events.

b)   A comet's tail, which is made up of evaporated gas and dust particles, is very bright.

c)   In 1705, Halley predicted the return of the comet that bears his name.

d)   Halley is only one person whose name has been used for a comet.

e)   The comet that is stitched on the Bayeux Tapestry was seen as an omen of doom for the Saxons at the Battle of Hastings in 1066.

2   Use these relative clauses in sentences.

a)   who was a famous explorer

_____

_____

b)   which came first in the international race

_____

_____

c)   that I did not know about

_____

_____

d)   whom we all know and love

_____

_____

Sentence construction

The paragraph below describes the crowds of people moving along the narrow streets of the old castle town of Mont St. Michel in France. The people's movements are said to be like water moving in a stream. Use the words in the box to complete the passage.

eddies   stream   water   floating   current   swirling   swept

The streets of the old city wandered at all angles up the steep side of the

hill upon which it was built. Like _____ in a _____,

the crowds of people moved along the streets, stopping and

_____ in little _____ around the souvenir stalls, while

the main _____ of people _____ towards the citadel.

Mont St. Michel in high summer was more to be endured than admired.

Yet from a distance, and because of the spindrift, the old castle town

seemed to be _____ above the sea.

Punctuation

Years are usually written in numerals.

1   Circle the years in this paragraph.

The sightings of comets had been recorded in 240 BCE and in CE 1066,

but it was not until 1705 that the return of one was predicted.

Edmund Halley (1656–1742), an English astronomer and

mathematician, said that the comet seen in 1682 was the same as the

one last seen in 1531 and 1607. He predicted that the comet would

return in late 1758 or early 1759. The comet returned in 1759. Since

then it has returned in 1835, 1910 and 1986.

2 Rewrite the paragraph using numerals where necessary.

In nineteen fifty-six, the Olympic Games were held in Melbourne. In nineteen ninety-six they were held in Atlanta, Georgia. Barcelona was the site for the Games in nineteen ninety-two. Los Angeles hosted the Games in nineteen eighty-four.

_____

_____

_____

Word knowledge

SPELL CHECK

Learn these words. Look, say, cover, write and check. Repeat until the word is spelled correctly.

axle	style	bundle	bustle	measles	miracle
attach	attempt	admitted	mattress	address	progress

1 Write the words in your spelling list and test yourself.
2 Write the words in sentences.

Write the correct form of the words in brackets.

1 The man _____ (admit) to the crime and _____ (attempt) to escape.

2 The clothes were _____ (bundle) up, _____ (wrap) in

paper and _____ (address) to the woman.

Over to you

(You may want to review the "Writing Process" on page 3.)
Comets and eclipses have been regarded by our ancestors as omens of doom. We know today that these events occur normally in space, and do not have to be connected with human events. Consult your encyclopedias and then write brief reports about each of the following: lunar eclipse, solar eclipse, comet, shooting star.

Map reading: China

Look at the map of China and answer the questions.

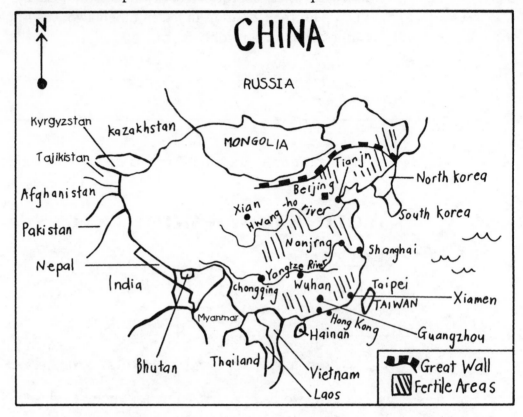

1 In what part of the country would you find the capital city, Beijing?

_____

2 What are the names of the cities near Hong Kong?

_____

3 Name five cities that are also major ports for world trade with China.

_____

_____

4 Which river valley is one of the largest and most fertile in the world?

_____

5 China's largest city (18 million people) is located near the mouth of the Yangtze River. Which city is that?

_____

6 The largest river in China is the Yangtze (known in China as the Changjiang). Three other large Chinese cities are located on this river. What are they?

_____

7 In what directions would you find the deserts of China?

_____

8 "Beijing" is Chinese for "Northern Capital." "Nan" is the Chinese word for "south." Which city is also known as the "Southern Capital?"

_____

9 What is the name of the very large manufacturing city and port near Beijing?

_____

10 List the countries that share a common border with China.

_____

_____

_____

Grammar

The past tense

When you write about contemporary cities, people and geographic features of a country, you normally use the present tense. We write about these places because they exist today.

Cross out the four incorrect verbs and write the correct verb above. Change only those verbs needed to make sense.

The ancient capital city of China was Xian, but the modern capital was Beijing. The Palace Museum is in Beijing, and an hour away by road there was the Great Wall of China at Badaling.

The Yangtze River was the biggest river in China, winding from Tibet to the Pacific Ocean through many provinces. This river, just like other Chinese rivers, floods the surrounding plains.

The Hwang-Ho is also called the Yellow River because it carried yellow soil from its upper reaches across northern China to the sea.

Sentence construction

Rewrite the sentences so that they make sense.

Hint: Start each sentence with the clause that begins after the comma, then use the conjunction in brackets to help you finish the sentence.
Example Walking along the road, the car almost ran over the dog. (as)
The car almost ran over the dog as it was walking down the road.

1   Having travelled all day by bus, the hotel was a welcome change for the passengers. (who)

_____

_____

2   Eating muesli with honey and yogourt, the dog watched Annie at breakfast. (as)

_____

_____

3   Reading the latest novel in the series, the dog could not understand why Jonathon was laughing. (as)

_____

_____

Punctuation

The colon (:) is used when you want to introduce a list of items or things into the text in a different way. (Note that the comma is also used as you present the list.)
Example
There were eight major cities noted on the map of China: Beijing, Shanghai, Hong Kong, Nanjing, Guangzhou, Tianjin, Wuhan and Chongqing.

Add a colon and commas to the following sentences. Don't forget capital letters where they are needed.

1 There are many famous ingredients in French cooking dijon mustard Boursault cheese French tarragon and Rothschild wine.

2 There are many famous dishes in Chinese cooking black mushrooms beijing duck bok choy pink ginger and sichuan beef.

Word knowledge

SPELL CHECK

Learn these words. Look, say, cover, write and check. Repeat until the word is spelled correctly.

motion   portion   conclusion   union   region   vision
aboard   hoarse   revenge   frequently   hectares   division

1 Write the words in your spelling list and test yourself.
2 Write the words in sentences.

Over to you

(You may want to review the "Writing Process" on page 3.)

1 Use an encyclopedia to help you match the following Chinese persons with their most remembered or honoured achievements or activities.

1	Confucius	**a**	finished the Great Wall
2	Lao Tzu	**b**	provincial Governor under Kublai Khan
3	Sun Tzu	**c**	the Empress Dowager
4	Emperor Chi	**d**	great philosopher (Kongzhi)
5	Mao Zedong	**e**	last Manchu Emperor
6	Ci Qi	**f**	founder of Tao religion
7	Pu Yi	**g**	famous Mongolian Emperor of China
8	Qianlong	**h**	emperor, poet, built Summer Palace
9	Kublai Khan	**i**	Chinese leader after 1949
10	Marco Polo	**j**	great Chinese general and writer

2 Chinese cooking is very popular throughout the world. Find a recipe book or a menu from a Chinese take-out restaurant and make a list of some of the vegetables used in Chinese cooking.

Informal notes

Congratulations

There are many times when we can write to people and congratulate them on something that has happened in their lives. Printed greeting cards can be used. People write a personal message inside the card. A written personal note always stands out as something special, and shows that the writer finds time to remember a friend.

1 Read this birthday note sent to a friend.

> November 19, 2005
>
> Dear Judy
> Happy Birthday to you. Happy Birthday to you.
> I thought that you would rather me write to you than sing to you!
> Have a fantastic day and keep away from the yummy, yummy chocolate cake.
>
> Your friend,
> Mai

2 Write a note with a birthday greeting to a class member.

Date _____

Dear _____

Write a paragraph or three sentences.

_____

_____

_____

_____

_____

_____

Signed _____

"Thank you" notes

"Thank you" notes are sent to people who have:
- given you a present
- done you a special favour
- had you stay at their house
- given you hospitality.

Write and send them a note as soon as possible after the favour has been done. Express your thanks simply and with sincerity.
Be straightforward and brief.

Read this "thank you" note Damien wrote to his grandparents for the birthday present they sent. Then write a "thank you" note to your local member of parliament who has been helpful to you.

March 12, 2005

Dear Nan and Pop,
Thank you for the two CDs you gave me for my birthday.
I had been saving up to buy them.
You always know what I want.

Hugs and kisses,
Damien

_____

_____

_____

_____

_____

_____

_____

_____

Grammar

Tense: infinitive, simple past, present participle, past participle

The base form of the verb is the infinitive, and is shown with **to** in front.
Example to eat, to run, to sleep, to be

The simple past tense of the verb makes us think of something that has happened in the past.
Example I **ate** lunch and **drank** some juice.

The present continuous tense makes us think of something that is still happening and not finished. This tense uses **am/is/are** with the present participle.
Example I **am going**. She **is swimming**. They **are playing**.

You can write a verb in the past tense by using the past participle with **has** or **have**.
Example I **have eaten** the apples.

1 Complete this chart with the principal parts of these verbs.

Infinitive	Simple past tense	Present participle	Past participle
to eat	ate	eating	eaten
to play	_____	playing	played
to keep	kept	keeping	_____
to speak	_____	speaking	spoken
to finish	finished	_____	finished

2 In the following sentences, circle the verbs which are written in the infinitive, simple past tense, present participle or past participle. Note: Verbs using the present participle and past participle always have two parts. *Example* is eating   had eaten

a) He is playing by the gate.

b) The man kept his washers in a tin.

c) The woman has played for Canada.

d) The boys are speaking together.

Punctuation

A period is used after abbreviations for the months of the year.

January	Jan.	* July	July
February	Feb.	August	Aug.
March	Mar.	September	Sept.
April	Apr.	October	Oct.
* May	May	November	Nov.
* June	June	December	Dec.

(* May, June and July should not be abbreviated.)

Proofread the sentences for periods that have been incorrectly used or left out. Make the corrections.

1 On Aug 1 1999 my mother told us her birthday was Oct 24 1970. We were interested and asked her some questions.
2 Was Grandma married on May. 30 1940?
3 Was Uncle Tom born July. 17 1971?
4 Is it true you first met Dad on Feb 19 1991?
5 Is Betsy's birthday June. 4 1978?

Word knowledge

SPELL CHECK

Learn these words. Look, say, cover, write and check. Repeat until the word is spelled correctly.

adult	canvas	bandage	tomatoes	medical	musical
tropical	chemical	carnival	interval	annual	material

1 Write the words in your spelling list and test yourself.
2 Write the words in sentences.

Over to you

(You may want to review the "Writing Process" on page 3.)
1 Read your local paper. Find an article that you think is well written and researched. Write to the editor with your congratulations.
2 Write a letter congratulating yourself on your recent achievements.

Putting a poem together

Write a poem with the title "Happiness is …"
Write about things that you know and like. Choose some ideas from the
box below, and give each topic a line in your poem. Add a few words or
ideas to each topic.

holidays vacation birthdays clothes camping pets my pet
favourite food   second most favourite food   favourite drink
favourite movie TV show games winning friends friendship
sharing place time of day plants favourite person

Here is an example.
Happiness is …
coconut ice cream on a hot summer's day
a friend walking with me on a beach
the joy of a remembered birthday
the re-run of a favourite movie
or watching "Survivor" on TV
the golden sun of a brand new day
and the stillness of the forest at night
all shared with friends and family.

_____

_____

_____

_____

_____

_____

_____

_____

_____

Choose a topic

The most important feature of a poem is the quality of the originality and creativity that the poet brings to the poem. Poems have been written about any topic you can imagine.

Choose something about which you would like to write a poem.

Write at least four lines. Your poem does not need to rhyme and can take any form you like. Here is an example.

Going the other way
The cars flash past in the night
carrying invisible people to places I cannot know;
lights rush at us, picking up the flashing white lines
that mercifully keep us apart.

_____

_____

_____

_____

_____

Using similes

The simile is a figure of speech. Speakers use similes every day. A person may be as hard as steel or as sharp as a tack. The simile takes a word and compares it to another word by using the words **like** and **as ... as**. Write a poem by completing the simile in each line below. (There are no wrong answers.)

Super similes

As fast as a _____

As strong as _____

Like a _____

And as kind as _____

Term 1

Narrative

Read the story and answer the questions.

Ulysses shipwrecked

Ulysses, one of the Greek heroes who fought at the siege of Troy, set sail for Ithaca, his native land. Once at sea, trouble came upon him. Storm followed storm and his small vessel was tossed upon the angry waves for many days. A mighty wave splintered the ship and Ulysses was cast upon the shore of a strange country.

Ulysses was found on the shore by the king's daughter. She took him to the palace where he was hospitably received by the king. A great feast was made in Ulysses' honour, and the chiefs of the land were invited .

After the feast the company moved to watch the games in which young men ran races, wrestled, boxed, threw rings and leapt over bars. The king's son Euryalus asked Ulysses to take part and forget his sorrows.

Ulysses put aside his cloak and took up a ring heavier than any thrown by the youths. He hurled it through the air far beyond where any other had thrown it that day.

Now all the spectators were amazed, and Ulysses said: "Match this throw who can. If anyone wishes, I will wrestle and box with him." They were all silent. The king ordered the minstrels to sing again.

The king commanded the chiefs to give the hero rich presents. As the gifts were presented, a chief minstrel sang of the Greek heroes and one called Ulysses. Ulysses wept.

The king spoke, "Hide not from us who you are, stranger. Tell by what name you are known in your own country." Ulysses replied: "O King, I am Ulysses! Ithaca is my home and that is where I would wish to be."

After a great silence, the king commanded his chiefs to hoist sail on their fastest vessel and send Ulysses on his way. Ulysses, taking his rich presents, set sail for his beloved Ithaca.

1   What does "storm followed storm" mean?

_____

2   For what place was Ulysses bound?

_____

3   Why were the young men silent after Ulysses had shown his skill?

_____

Report

Read the report and draw an illustration for each paragraph. Write a sentence under each explaining the illustration.

Disappearing icebergs: where do they go?

Icebergs are huge masses of ice which have broken away from the edge of an ice sheet or glacier and float on the ocean. Only about one ninth of an iceberg is above the surface of the water. Icebergs are found in the Arctic and Antarctic oceans. Greenland, in the northern hemisphere, is the source of most of the icebergs in the North Atlantic.

In April 1912, the British liner, *Titanic*, on its maiden voyage and thought to be unsinkable, collided with an iceberg in the North Atlantic and sank with a huge loss of life. Since 1914, shipping lanes are patrolled and the location of icebergs is reported to any ship in the vicinity.

Icebergs drift from the Antarctic, but as there are few ships in the vicinity they cause little trouble.

Where do icebergs go? They melt away slowly as the upper part is warmed by the sun and the lower part is warmed by warmer waters.

Transaction

Read this report. Write questions as headings before each paragraph.
You will need four questions.

Tears

1 _____

Tears are made of salt water. If you have ever licked your fingers after
wiping away your tears, you would have tasted salt. Tears happen
when the gland that produces moisture to keep the eyeball rotating
properly makes more water than usual. The eye is unable to drain this
extra water away, so a flood of tears occurs.

2 _____

Tears are produced by a gland called the lachrymal gland (*lacryma* is
the Latin word for tear). The gland is about the size of an almond
shell and is found above the eye.

3 _____

Each time a person blinks, water is spread over the eye by six or more
little ducts. Extra water is collected by two little canals at the inner
corner of the eye where the upper and lower eyelids join.

4 _____

When the tear gland is stimulated by a pungent smell, such as
detergents, household ammonia, onions, or by a happy or sad event,
the tear duct makes more water than usual.

Letter writing

Write an informal note of congratulations to a member of your class who has won a prize in a story writing competition.

(Date) _____

Dear _____

_____

_____

_____

_____

_____

_____

_____

_____

_____

_____

_____

_____

(Closure) _____

(Signed) _____

Excalibur

Read the text and match the information in the columns on the next page.

King Arthur's mighty sword, the one he pulled from the stone to become king, was broken in battle. The magic that brought him that sword returned to bring him Excalibur. This is the story of Excalibur.

Arthur was riding beside the lake with Merlin when they saw an arm, clothed in white and sword in hand, appear from the surface of the lake. Arthur paddled a small boat to the arm as the Lady of the Lake appeared from the mist and gave him permission to take the sword, which she called Excalibur. She said that he must return it at some time in the future.

Excalibur proved to be a mighty sword, and Arthur performed great deeds in battle. After many years, he and his knights found themselves at war with the evil Mordred and his rebel knights. The final battle of that war was fought near the magic lake, and almost all of the knights were killed. Arthur was mortally wounded.

Sir Bedevere was only partly injured, but Arthur knew that he was fit enough to undertake the task of returning the sword to the Lady of the Lake. He told Bedevere to throw Excalibur into the lake. Bedevere took the sword, but he changed his mind as he went to the lake. He hid the sword because he wanted it for himself.

When he returned, Arthur asked him what had happened as he threw Excalibur into the lake. Bedevere replied that nothing had happened, so Arthur ordered him to recover the sword from its hiding place and throw it into the lake. Even though Arthur was dying, Bedevere now knew that he could not disobey him. He ran to the sword, picked it up and hurled it into the lake.

The moonlight reflected from the whirling blade in silver flashes, and as it came close to the surface an arm appeared from the water and took the sword by the hilt. Excalibur disappeared into the lake without a ripple, its point being the last thing that Bedevere saw.

Sir Bedevere could now tell Arthur what had happened. Excalibur had been returned properly. Arthur died some hours later, and his body was taken onto a magic boat, which then disappeared silently into the mist.

Match the items in Column A with the explanations in Column B.

Column A	Column B
1 Excalibur	**a** leader of the knights who opposed Arthur
2 Sir Bedevere	**b** King Arthur's magician and teacher
3 Mordred	**c** modern name of town near the Lake
4 Merlin	**d** tournaments where knights "play" at fighting
5 The Lady of the Lake	**e** one of the last of Arthur's knights
6 The Round Table	**f** King Arthur's sword
7 King Arthur	**g** story using myth and fantasy
8 Glastonbury	**h** the keeper of Excalibur
9 legend	**i** the group of knights whom King Arthur led
10 the lists or tourney	**j** legendary King of the Britons

Grammar

Noun–pronoun agreement and the verbs *am, is, are, was, were*

The pronoun used after these verbs has the same case (subjective) as the pronoun or noun before the verb.
Example **He** is taller than **I**.
That **girl** is faster than **I**.
Tip: Finish the sentence to find if a verb has been left off. In both sentences above, the final word left off is the verb **am**.
Example He is taller than I (am).
Note: Many people say **me** in general, everyday spoken English.

Choose the correct pronouns to complete the sentences. (Don't forget the tip: Can you finish the sentence by adding a missing verb?)

1 The new gardener works harder than _____. (her, she)

2 All children in the class were as good as _____. (he, him)

3 All the children in the class were studying for _____. examination. (they, them, their, theirs)

4 The stallion was faster than _____. (it, him)

Comparative degree of adverbs

The comparative degree of the adverb is used when comparing two things.
Example The flamingo lands **more gracefully** than the albatross.

Complete the sentences using a form of the adverb in brackets. Note the use of **more**.

1 Shane bowls _____ than any other bowler in the world. (effectively)

2 The man drove the car _____ than ever on the winding mountain road. (dangerously)

3 Out in the kitchen, the chefs were preparing dinner _____ than ever before. (carefully)

Punctuation

Add commas where they are needed.

1 Patrick and Mei-ling went to the store and bought tomatoes basil three different kinds of lettuce French dressing and cheese.

2 Susan and Helena who are my first cousins are also good friends.

3 Last Saturday as we were riding our bikes we met some new kids near the video games plaza.

Word knowledge

SPELL CHECK

Learn these words. Look, say, cover, write and check. Repeat until the word is spelled correctly.

mining	lightning	therefore	neither	seized	weir
veiled	ceiling	height	eighth	whether	width

1 Write the words in your spelling list and test yourself.
2 Write the words in sentences.

1 Replace the word or phrase in *italics* with a word from the Spell Check.

a) The engineers constructed a *dam for storing water* _____ near the town.

b) The prisoner *took* _____ the gun from the policeman.

c) The mountains were *covered* _____ with dense mist.

d) What's the *altitude* _____ of the Empire State building?

Homonyms are words that sound the same or similarly but are spelled differently. They are frequently confused, causing spelling errors.

2 Look up the meaning of the following pairs of homonyms and write each correctly in a sentence.

board	boarder	its	die	hear	personal
bored	border	it's	dye	here	personnel

Over to you

1 Find out something about each of the following: Knights of the Round Table, Camelot, Guinevere, Morgana, Merlin, Lancelot, Sir Kay, Galahad, Mordred.
2 "The Once and Future King" is an inscription, originally in Latin, found on a stone in England. It is thought to have marked the gravesite of King Arthur. Other places connected with the King Arthur legend include Tintagel and Glastonbury. Find out more about these places and other places associated with the Arthurian legends.

Questionnaires

Pastimes

A pastime is an activity or hobby that you enjoy doing, something that helps you pass the time of day pleasantly.

People have many different pastimes: playing sport, darts, chess, cards, doing jigsaws, crossword puzzles, playing board games, driving, reading, watching television, computer games, walking and gardening. There are almost as many different pastimes as there are people. A great amount of time is spent at pastimes because they are enjoyable.

1 Use the questionnaire below to find the pastime of a friend or family member. You might like to pool your data, or some of it, with the data collected by other members of the class.

Questionnaire

Date _____

Name _____   Date of Birth _____

Gender _____   **Address (circle one)**

city/semi-rural/rural

1 What is your favourite pastime? _____
2 Circle how many hours you would spend at it in a normal week.
   >20   15–20   10–15   5–10   <5

3 Do you have other pastimes? Yes/No
4 List these in the space below.

_____

_____

5 How many hours would you spend on these in a normal week?
   >20   15–20   10–15   5–10   <5

6 Do you belong to a club for your favourite pastime?   Yes/No
7 What other pastimes would you like to do if you had time?

_____

8 Why is your favourite pastime so important to you?

_____

---

2 Answer these questions.

a) The word "pastime" is made from which two words?

_____

b) Why would people with the same pastime join a club?

_____

c) What word describes the information gained from research?

_____

d) What must researchers do about this information?

_____

e) What does "pooling data" mean?

_____

f) Remember to take the questionnaire yourself before giving it to others. What is your favourite pastime?

_____

Grammar

Subject groups

A subject group is a group of words that function together with the main noun before or after the verb. A subject group may be one word or many words. The subject groups in the following sentences are underlined for you.
<u>This bus</u> follows <u>the high road</u>.
<u>This bus</u> follows <u>the picturesque high road</u>.
<u>This bus</u> follows <u>the high road which follows the ridge</u>.

Underline the subject groups that appear before and after the main verb.

1 The old gentleman **tended** his wonderful garden every day.

2 The vegetables that he gave to friends **included** small butternut squash.

3 Massed herbs **presented** a picture of different greens and the bright colours of their small flowers.

4 Many vegetables and herbs **were growing** profusely.

Sentence construction

Sentences that are not completed, or that do not contain a finite or complete verb, are known as **sentence fragments**. Sentence fragments should not be used in reports, or in any formal writing.

Rewrite the sentence fragments so that they are complete or entire sentences.

Note: You may need to add further information to some of them.

1 Growing vegetables for his kitchen and his friends

_____

2 The coach telling them what to do

_____

3 Having driven from Toronto to Florida in two days

_____

4 Surfing the net because he wanted to

_____

Punctuation

Replace the **and** in these sentences with a semi-colon.

1 The children enjoyed their day at the beach and they really loved the nearby waterslide.

_____

_____

2 His favourite pastime was big-game fishing and he had the trophies to show for it.

_____

_____

3 Going to the movies to see Mel Gibson is great and so is watching Jodie Foster act.

_____

_____

Word knowledge

SPELL CHECK

Learn these words. Look, say, cover, write and check. Repeat until the word is spelled correctly.

attention   calendar   deny   disaster   easy   excel
favourite   forty   ghost   heavily   jewel   knight

1 Write the words in your spelling list and test yourself.
2 Write the words in sentences.

Replace the word or phrase in *italics* with a word from the Spell Check.

1 The exercise was *not difficult* _____ .

2 I could *not say* _____ that I had done it.

3 The *precious stone* _____ in the necklace was beautiful.

4 There was a *list of dates* _____ on the wall.

precious stone . . .

Over to you

(You may want to review the "Writing Process" on page 3.)
1 Devise a questionnaire about favourite TV shows. Test the questions on two people, and make any changes to your questions. Give the questionnaire to people from different age groups. Write a report of your findings.
2 Find out something about each of the following: poll, survey, Gallup, Ipsos-Reid Poll, sample, representative sample, sample bias.

Reading bus timetables

Look at the timetable and answer the questions.

To city

Depart	Bus stop locations	Monday - Friday					
Fruitgrove	Smith St. at Shopping Centre	7:25	7:40	7:55	8:10	8:30	9:00
Acadia	Browns Rd. and Gavin St.	7:28	7:43	7:58	8:13	8:33	9:13
Stanford	Browns Rd. and Rose Cres.	7:30	7:45	8:00	8:15	8:35	9:15
Newhaven	Browns Rd. at the Cineplex	7:34	7:49	8:04	8:19	8:39	9:19
Meadowvale	Sanctuary Rd. and Current Dr.	7:38	7:53	8:08	8:23	8:43	9:23
South Grove	Sanctuary Rd. and Main St.	7:40	7:55	8:10	8:25	8:45	9:25
City Centre	Main St. at Council Chambers	7:42	7:57	8:12	8:27	8:47	9:27

* Weekend services: buses leave on the hour, every hour, from Fruitgrove.

1   What is the earliest time that a bus departs from Meadowvale for the City Centre?

_____

2   The trip from Fruitgrove to the City takes 17 minutes (7:25 to 7:42). Which bus should Mrs. Green, of Fruitgrove, catch in order to meet an appointment in the city at 9 a.m.?

_____

3   How long does it normally take for a bus to get from Acadia to South Grove?

_____

4   How many bus services are provided between 7:15 and 9:00 on any weekday morning?

_____

5   How long does the bus take to get from Current Drive to the first Main Street stop?

_____

6   What do the following abbreviations mean: Dr., Cres., St., Rd.?

_____

Grammar

Could have

Many people say that they **could of been to** some place, or that they **should of done** or **need to of done** something.

In formal speaking, and in writing, the correct use is **could have**, **would have**, **should have** and **need to have**.

Read the passage and circle the five instances where **of** needs to be changed to **have**.

The children said that they could of caught the bus at eight o'clock but then they would of missed the connection with the train at North Bay Station. They needed to of boarded an earlier bus but that meant they would of had to get out of bed too early. The teacher said that they should of got out of bed when their mother had called them.

Sentence construction

Complete the clauses in each sentence.

1 We went to the Cineplex where _____

and afterwards missed the bus because _____.

2 The bus trip _____ Fruitgrove _____ the city

takes longer _____ there is too much traffic or when

_____.

3 The children went _____ where they met

_____ who asked _____.

Punctuation

The colon is used when you wish to introduce a long list into your writing. The colon follows the introduction to the list.

introduction

↓

Example There are many planets colder than Earth: Mars, Jupiter, Saturn, Uranus, Neptune and Pluto.

Write a list of zoo animals, using a colon at the end of the introduction to your list.

_____

_____

_____

_____

_____

Word knowledge

SPELL CHECK

Learn these words. Look, say, cover, write and check. Repeat until the word is spelled correctly.

presence	absence	defence	usually
gradually	generally	finally	connected
beginning	annoyed	engineer	pioneer

1 Write the words in your spelling list and test yourself.
2 Write the words in sentences.

1 Replace the word or phrase in *italics* with a word from the Spell Check.

a) The *person* _____ who designed the bridge was there.

b) My little brother *irritated* _____ me this morning.

c) Many buildings are *joined* _____ at first floor level.

d) *Last of all* _____ the best actor award was presented.

2 Circle the word that doesn't fit in each list.

a) radio, records, video, audio tapes

b) candle, lantern, lamp, switch

c) factory, kiosk, shop, store

Over to you

1 Collect bus and train timetables for the public transport services you would use in your city or town. Why is the information provided in columns? Draw up a simple timetable for your own use by listing only those stops that are important to your travel.
2 Survey the children in your class or in your school to find out:
   a) how many use public transport
   b) what kind of transport they use
   c) how often they use it in a two-week period
   d) what are their purposes for using public transport.
   Organize your information in a table.

A close encounter with Australian nature

Read the report and answer the questions.

Healesville Sanctuary is situated in the Yarra Valley in Victoria and is a 90-minute drive east from Melbourne. It is set in 31 hectares of natural bushland and contains over 200 species of Australian wildlife.

Breeding programs operate for more than 20 threatened Australian species. Those animals in the breeding program include the mountain pygmy possum, the long-footed potoroo and the helmeted honeyeater. The sanctuary also cares for hundreds of injured, orphaned or sick native animals and birds. Staff members care for these rescued creatures, restoring them to a healthy condition before releasing them into the wild.

The program for the day of our excursion included seeing platypuses, wombats, pelicans and reptiles. The various keepers explained to us why these creatures are important to Australia, how they live, what they eat, where they were found, and where they are now found.

Kangaroos and swamp wallabies hop around the sanctuary. Emus wander around feeding. In huge mesh-enclosed aviaries, native birds flew as we walked through. The best presentation was with the birds of prey. In a large enclosure in which the birds can fly, the specialist keepers told us about wedge-tailed eagles and peregrine falcons. The birds fly at noon and at 3 p.m. daily. I went and watched them both times.

There are two new exhibits at the sanctuary. One is the Sidney Myer World of the Platypus and the other is the Frog Bog which has snakes, tadpoles, water skinks, beetles and dragonflies living alongside the frogs.

At this sanctuary, animals and birds have large spaces in which to live and move around. With its green bushland setting, Healesville Sanctuary is nothing like the zoos of the past.

We had a picnic underneath the trees and I lost my bread roll to a very fast emu with a long neck. The trip back to Melbourne capped off a wonderful day.

1 What are the names of the new exhibits at the Sanctuary?

_____

2 Which exhibit did the writer enjoy most?

_____

3 List four animals seen at this zoo.

_____

4 What native birds did the writer see?

_____

5 Write the names of three threatened Australian species to be seen at the sanctuary.

_____

6 What do you feel about zoos and sanctuaries for birds and animals? Should we have them?

_____

_____

_____

_____

Grammar

Theme and rheme

Information in writing has to be presented so that readers can follow what the writer is saying. Writers and readers achieve understanding because the beginning of each clause states the theme or topic of the clause. The rest of the clause provides comment about that theme.

So a clause has two main parts: theme (topic) and rheme (comment).

Example   An eagle soared high into the air.
                        ↑   ↑
            theme (topic) **rheme** (comment)

Read the one-clause sentences. Underline the theme or topic. The first is done for you.

1 <u>Healesville Sanctuary</u> is situated in the Yarra Valley.

2 The sanctuary was started as a research institute in the 1920s.

3 Breeding programs operate for more than 20 threatened species.

4 The helmeted honeyeater is Victoria's official bird emblem.

5 Kangaroos and swamp wallabies hop around the sanctuary.

Sentence construction

A report on any matter uses words that can be grouped in the same category. For example, a report about traffic would use words like cars, trucks, roads, streets, parking, accidents, pavement, transit lanes, transport, buses, highway, freeway and so on.

Complete the text using all the words in the box.

Greek	bios	zoon	botanikos	zoologists	life
	biology	animal	botanist	zoology	

The word "zoo" is derived from the old Greek word _____

which means an _____ . The study of animals is called

_____ , and researchers studying the lives and habits of

animals are known as _____ . Zoology is part of the larger

study of _____ or living things called _____ . The

old Greek word _____ means life. Another scientific researcher

in biology is the _____ , who studies plants. Do you know

what the old _____ word _____ means?

Word knowledge

Learn these words. Look, say, cover, write and check. Repeat until the word is spelled correctly.

passenger	compass	medicine	imagine
submarine	separated	prepared	declared
poultry	soul	mould	boulder

1 Write the words in your spelling list and test yourself.
2 Write the words in sentences.

1 Replace the word or phrase in italics with a word from the Spell Check.

   a) The *underwater vessel* _____ rose to the surface.

   b) An *instrument for determining direction* _____ was put in the boat.

   c) The children were *cut off* _____ from their parents.

   d) The chef *got ready* _____ for her television program.

2 Circle the word that doesn't fit in each list.

   a) roof, dome, gutter, pergola

   b) envelope, wrapper, book, shrink-wrap

   c) letter, messenger, herald, courier

   d) ship, submarine, boat, airplane

Over to you

(You may want to review the "Writing Process" on page 3.)
1 Write to your provincial or territorial tourism department asking them for any information they may have about local wildlife sanctuaries and zoos. Use your information to write a report about wildlife sanctuaries and zoos in Canada.

High jump: scissors style

Read the explanation and rules, then answer the questions.

The scissors-style jump is used by many elementary school students. The scissors is a good style because it:

- indicates natural spring
- trains students to use natural spring in take-off
- provides a comfortable and balanced landing position.

Teaching points

- Practise run-up to the same take-off point for each jump.
- Must use a short run.
- Must approach the bar on an angle.
- Must practise take-off.
- Must use straight knee to gain upward momentum.
- Must swing arms upward.
- Must scissor legs as they cross the bar.
- Must land comfortably on lead leg first.

Competition rules

1 Competitors must take off using one foot.
2 Knocking the bar off counts as failure.
3 Posts shall not be moved during the competition. (Unless the referee decides the ground has become unsafe.)
4 Competitors may choose to miss a turn and try for the next height.
5 Competitors are eliminated after three successive failures, regardless of the height.
6 If the last two jumpers are tied at the same height, the competitor with the lowest total of failures in the competition up to and including the height last jumped may be awarded first place.

1   How should a competitor land from a scissors-style high jump?

_____

2   Who is judged the winner of a high jump competition if there is a tie on the last height?

_____

_____

3   Why do the rules forbid shifting the posts once competition has started?

_____

_____

4   Why use a short run-up?

_____

5   What happens if a competitor misses a turn at a lower jump and clears the bar when it has been set at a higher level?

_____

Sentence construction

Change the tense of the verb in bold from past to present tense.

1   The dogs **looked** suspiciously at the food; the mother dog **began** to eat.

_____

_____

2   My sister **tried** to open the door.

_____

3   I **parked** my bike under the tree and **walked** inside.

_____

4   The group **picked** up their lunch at the buffet and then **sat** down and **ate**.

_____

_____

Grammar

Active/Passive voice

1 Rewrite the sentences to change the voice of the verb (underlined) from the passive to the active. The first is done for you.

    a) The American jumper must <u>have been beaten</u> by the Canadian.
    → The Canadian must <u>have beaten</u> the American jumper.

    b) The bar <u>must</u> only <u>be set</u> by the officials.

    _____

    c) The bar <u>must be approached</u> on an angle by the jumper.

    _____

    d) The officials <u>have been thanked</u> by the athletes.

    _____

2 Rewrite the sentences, changing the voice of the verb (underlined) from the active to the passive. The first one is done for you.

    a) The athletes <u>enjoyed</u> the meals at the games. → The meals at the games <u>were enjoyed</u> by the athletes.

    b) The courteous officials <u>helped</u> the athletes.

    _____

    c) The jumpers <u>must jump</u> off one foot.

    _____

    d) Talent scouts from all over the world <u>may observe</u> the athletes.

    _____

Word knowledge

SPELL CHECK

Learn these words. Look, say, cover, write and check. Repeat until the word is spelled correctly.

they're	you're	investigated	debated
decorate	gracefully	tire	retired
requirement	fortunately	inquired	siren

1 Write the words in your spelling list and test yourself.
2 Write the words in sentences.

1 Replace the word or phrase in *italics* with a word from the Spell Check.

   a) Many people like to *dress up* _____ their houses for special holidays.

   b) At the hospital we *asked* _____ after the patient's health.

   c) The two groups *argued* _____ that capital punishment was wrong.

   d) The dancers moved *elegantly* _____ across the stage.

2 Homonyms are words that sound the same or similarly but are spelled differently. The are frequently confused, which results in spelling errors. Look up the meaning of the following pairs of homonyms and write each correctly in a sentence.

| brake | plain | desert | their | human |
| break | plane | dessert | there | humane |

Over to you

1 Rewrite the "Competition Rules" (p. 46) changing the voice of each verb from active to passive.
2 Which voice—active or passive—sounds better for stating rules? Why?

Formal party invitation

1 Read this formal invitation and look at the features it has.

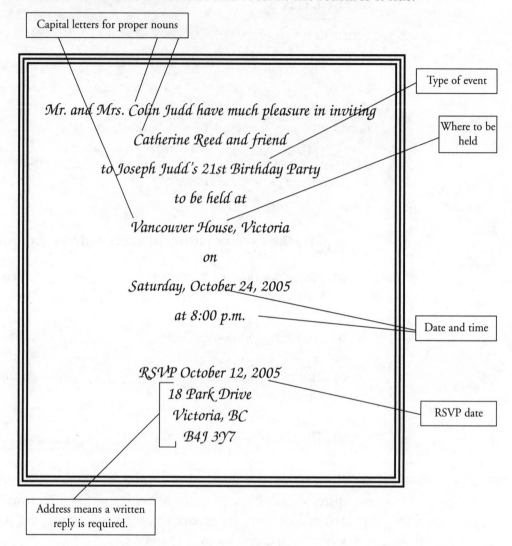

Capital letters for proper nouns

Type of event

Where to be held

Mr. and Mrs. Colin Judd have much pleasure in inviting

Catherine Reed and friend

to Joseph Judd's 21st Birthday Party

to be held at

Vancouver House, Victoria

on

Saturday, October 24, 2005

at 8:00 p.m.

Date and time

RSVP October 12, 2005

18 Park Drive

Victoria, BC

B4J 3Y7

RSVP date

Address means a written reply is required.

RSVP is the only shortened form of a word (or acronym) used in a formal invitation. It is French for *repondez s'il vous plait,* which means "please reply."

2 On a separate page write a formal invitation from your parent/s inviting your friend to your birthday party. Write one paragraph, using the following guidelines:

- Give type of event, where to be held, date and time, and RSVP date.
- Include your address.
- Do not use contractions.
- Use capital letters for proper nouns.

A formal reply

1 Look at the features of a formal reply.

Capital letters for proper nouns

Type of event

Catherine Reed and Charles Windsor have much pleasure in accepting
the kind invitation of Mr and Mrs Colin Judd to Joseph Judd's
21st Birthday Party to be held at Vancouver House,
Victoria on Saturday, October 24, 2005 at 8:00 p.m.

2A Pine Drive
Victoria, BC
B6A 4H2

Where to
be held

Your address

Date and time

2 Write a formal reply from your friend accepting your parents'
invitation to your birthday party.
Write one paragraph, using the following guidelines:
- Give type of event, where to be held, date and time, RSVP date.
- Include your address.
- Do not use contractions.
- Use capital letters for proper nouns.

_____

_____

_____

_____

_____

Addressing an envelope

Remember to check that you have the full address (name, street, town,
postal code) and use a title for the person. Add the three items missing
from this address.

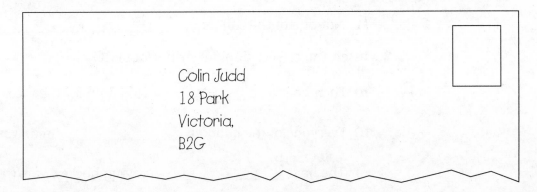

Colin Judd
18 Park
Victoria,
B2G

Grammar

each every none anybody everybody nobody

These words must be followed by verbs in the singular.

The singular verbs are in **bold**.
Complete the sentences.

1 Every person **has** _____.

2 None of the fruit **was** _____.

3 Each car **was** _____.

4 Nobody **is** _____.

5 Anybody **is** _____.

6 Everybody **was** _____.

each of one of neither of either of not one of every one of

These expressions must be followed by verbs in the singular.

1 Use a singular verb and complete each sentence:

   a) Each of the girls _____.

   b) Every one of _____.

   c) One of the men _____.

   d) Neither of the contestants _____.

   e) Either of the sisters _____.

   f) Not one of the sailors _____.

2 Insert the correct singular or plural verb.

   a) Each horse _____ lined up for the race. was/were

   b) Everyone of the balloons _____ red. was/were

   c) The boys _____ playing hockey. was/were

Word knowledge

SPELL CHECK

Learn these words. Look, say, cover, write and check. Repeat until the word is spelled correctly.

arrival	unusual	funeral	special
hospital	quality	altered	altogether
suitable	comfortable	capable	valuable

1 Write the words in your spelling list and test yourself.
2 Write the words in sentences.

An anagram is a word that is made by moving a letter or letters of one word to make another word.
Example **snip** becomes **pins**

Write the anagram of the words in the table.

	clue	anagram
lips	a sudden movement	s _____
pane	the back of the neck	n _____
stop	used to cook in	p _____
reap	a fruit	p _____

Over to you

(You may want to review the "Writing Process" on page 3.)

1 You have received an invitation from the Premier of your province to the opening of Parliament. Write a formal reply accepting the invitation.
2 Dogs are not supposed to like mail deliverers. Do you think this is true or false? In a paragraph state your ideas.

Forms of poetry

There are some popular forms of poetry. Among the most popular are the haiku, senryu, tanka and the limerick.

Haiku and senryu

The haiku (pronounced high-koo in English) is a three-line poem of 17 syllables about nature. The last line contains some thought or feeling about life and nature.

Sunset
The day ends in red   (5 syllables)
Stretching across horizons (7 syllables)
Into the future. (5 syllables)

Write your own haiku, one or more, about sunrise, trees, sleep, frogs, bees, crows or any topic of your choice. Remember to follow the pattern of 5–7–5 syllables for the three lines. There is no need to rhyme.

_____

_____

_____

_____

The senryu (pronounced sen-dyoo in English) has the same pattern as the haiku, can be about any topic, but does not need to have a theme about nature or a comment on life.

Basketball
The big man takes off (5 syllables)
Flying through opposition (7 syllables)
Alley-oop! Slam dunk! (5 syllables)

Write your own senryu.

_____

_____

_____

_____

Tanka

The tanka (pronounced tang-ka) is another Japanese form poem. It has 31 syllables in five lines in the order 5–7–5–7–7. The same rules apply as for haiku.

Sunset

A black disc above (5 syllables)
the mountain in the distance (7 syllables)
Sheds red and orange (5 syllables)
Across the sky and through night (7 syllables)
As the moon stalks her old prey. (7 syllables)

Write a tanka of your own on a separate page.

Limerick

The limerick has five lines and a particular rhyme and rhythm.
Look at the rhyme in this limerick.   Now listen to the rhythm.

There was a young man from the town	**1**	~/~~/~~/ (three strong beats: ///)
Who decided to pay half a crown	**2**	~~/~~/~~/ (three strong beats: ///)
For a ride on a swing;	**3**	~~/~~/ (two strong beats: //)
But he fell off the thing	**4**	~~/~~/ (two strong beats: //)
So instead of up he went down.	**5**	~~/~/~~/ (three strong beats: ///)

Lines 1, 2 and 5 rhyme: town, crown and down. Lines 3 and 4 rhyme: swing and thing.
Write your own limerick about a person from any place you know. Plenty of rhymes can be made from words and places that end in: ate, ight, ite, ote, an, ar, or, erth, oat, out, eight, ort and so on.

_____

_____

_____

_____

Term 2

Report

Read the report and answer the questions.

Craig Kielburger was 12 years old in 1996 and living in Thornhill, Ontario, when he read a newspaper article about a 12-year-old boy in Pakistan who was murdered for speaking out against child labour. Iqbal Masik had been sold into slavery as a carpet weaver when he was four years old.

Stunned by what had happened to this Pakistani boy, Craig, at age 14, travelled with a human rights worker to South Asia and saw the child labour for himself. Children from a young age are enslaved in carpet-making factories and forced to work under terrible conditions. They have no hope of ever going to school. Craig also learned that these carpets are imported into Canada and other countries. He wrote his first book "Free the Children" about his trip.

Distressed that no one was speaking out on behalf of these children, Craig organized his friends and classmates and founded "Free the Children." This organization was and still is funded by garage sales, pop sales, car washes, and bake sales. No one who sits on its board of directors is over the age of 18.

By 1998, this organization had raised enough money from classroom donations to pay for a rehabilitation centre for Pakistani children who have escaped slavery.

"Free the Children" is dedicated to bringing the plight of children who work in the sweatshops in South Asia to the public's attention. This organization is working to have carpets that are imported to Canada labelled to identify those not made by children. This is one way of stopping child enslavement in South Asia.

1   What incident got Craig involved in his work on behalf of enslaved children?

_____

2   What is the name of the organization that Craig founded with his friends?

_____

3   State two things that are unusual about this organization.

_____

4   How will labelling carpets that are imported into Canada and not made by children help solve the child labour problem in South Asia?

_____

Transaction

Devise a questionnaire with six questions to find out what people like to do in their leisure or free time. Correct punctuation and spelling must be used. Use this format for your questionnaire.

Questionnaire

Name: _____ Date: _____

Gender: _____ Date of Birth: _____

1 _____

2 _____

3 _____

4 _____

5 _____

6 _____

Procedure

Choose an activity that you like to perform such as skipping or hopping. Write how you perform the activity using no more than six steps. Think about it and draw rough sketches to help you before you start.

1 _____

2 _____

3 _____

4 _____

5 _____

6 _____

Explanation

1 Read the text.

Have you ever wondered why animals need oxygen?

Every living animal needs oxygen to live. Animal cells need oxygen to convert fuel to energy and every cell must get rid of its gaseous waste (carbon dioxide).

In simple animals each cell gets oxygen for itself. In more highly developed animals, a special mechanism exchanges oxygen and carbon dioxide on behalf of the whole body. The blood in the circulatory system carries oxygen and the respiratory system carries away the waste.

Are humans still water-dwelling creatures?

We carry our watery environment around with us inside our skins. Because humans have lungs instead of gills, they are able to live on land. To do this the air must be rich in oxygen.

How abundant is oxygen?

Oxygen is the most abundant element on Earth and forms about half of the total material of the Earth's surface. It makes up one fifth by volume of air, about 90 per cent of water and two-thirds of the human body.

What are the uses of oxygen?

Oxygen is used in medicine for the treatment of respiratory diseases and is mixed with other gases for respiration in submarines, high flying aircraft and spacecraft. It is also mixed with other gases for industrial and manufacturing purposes.

2 Draw four diagrams using the headings in the text. Write a sentence under each diagram.

Scott of the Antarctic

Read the story and answer the questions.

Captain Robert Falcon Scott (1868–1912) was born in Devonport in England. He joined the Royal Navy as a midshipman at the age of 14, and by 1900 had attained the rank of Commander, RN.

Scott led two expeditions to the Antarctic. On his second trip he set out to become the first person to reach the South Pole. With three companions, Scott pulled heavy sleighs across the polar plateau. This story concerns the last days of this expedition in which Scott, Oates, Wilson and Bowers perished on their return journey from the South Pole, and is taken from the last leaves in Scott's diary.

By Friday, March 16, 1912, Scott and his companions were stranded by a blizzard and were almost out of food. They were not far from a depot where food and fuel were stored, but they had a series of disasters. They were suffering illness, hunger and frostbite, and the blizzards made further travel almost impossible.

Titus Oates had borne intense pain for some weeks, but one night he expected to die. He awoke the next morning in terrible agony, and left the tent to walk to his death in the blizzard.

The continuing blizzard made it impossible to reach the depot. The group's food and fuel was almost gone, and now fierce gales lashed up the snow so much that travel became impossible. Food and fuel ran out as they waited for the weather to clear.

Eight months later, in November 1912, the rescue party found their bodies. Scott had been the last to die, and under his shoulders was a wallet containing his three diaries.

The diaries showed that Scott's party had reached the South Pole on January 18, 1912 to find that the Norwegian explorer, Roald Amundsen, had beaten them to the South Pole by a month.

1 What is meant by the expression "the last leaves" of a book or diary?

_____

2 How old was Scott when he became a Commander in the British Navy?

_____

3 What natural events brought great problems to the expedition on the return journey?

_____

4 Why did Oates give his life away?

_____

5 Apart from the intense cold, a major problem is carrying sufficient provisions for an expedition. Which items are mentioned three times in the text?

_____

Grammar

Incomplete clauses

The following sentences begin with incomplete clauses. Some of them do not make sense. Turn all of the incomplete clauses into complete clauses by shifting the incomplete clause to the end of the sentence and making the changes needed, using the conjunction supplied. The first one is done for you.

1 Carrying insufficient fuel, the tents could not be heated and the men froze. (because) → The tents could not be heated and the men froze because they carried insufficient fuel.

2 Leaving the tent while the others were asleep, the rest of the expedition did not know that Titus Oates had gone. (when)

_____

_____

3 Having travelled slowly for many days in the blizzard, the tents were put up for the last time. (after)

_____

_____

4 To be the first person to travel to the South Pole and back alive, the expedition was led by Robert Scott. (who)

_____

_____

Adjectives

Combine the sentences using the comparative or superlative form of the adjective in brackets.

1   Scott's second expedition to the South Pole was fateful. They were

caught by the _____ (bad) blizzards they could have ever experienced.

2   Amundsen's journey to the South Pole was _____ (fast) than

Scott's. He had left _____ (early) than Scott and met

_____ (few) blizzards.

3   Most of the Antarctic land mass is covered by thick layers of ice and

snow. The _____ (thick) layers are those that are

_____ (far) from the oceans that surround the icy continent.

Punctuation

Place the commas in the correct places in the following sentences (if they are needed).
1   Driving the old car along the road we were passed by many other cars.
2   Because we had read the book and enjoyed it we could not wait to see the movie.
3   Running aground in the boat was not appreciated by its owner.
4   We had tried to buy the horse which was a bay mare but did not have enough money.
5   If the children wanted to visit the museum then they had to book their visit some months in advance.

Word knowledge

SPELL CHECK

Learn these words. Look, say, cover, write and check. Repeat until the word is spelled correctly.

brooch	boomerang	lagoon	cockatoo
drought	thoroughly	introduced	prefer
laughter	conquer	period	average

1 Write the words in your spelling list and test yourself.
2 Write the words in sentences.

1 Read the word in Column A. Match it up with the word in Column B.

Column A	**Column B**
lagoon	ordinary
conquer	a portion of time
average	overcome
period	a freshwater lake

2 Rewrite the correct form of the words in brackets.

a) The woman said she _____ (prefer) a cockatoo as a pet.

b) The machine washed the clothes _____ (thorough).

c) The baseball player _____ (average) eight runs per inning.

d) I _____ (introduce) the minister to the audience.

Over to you

(You may want to review the "Writing Process" on page 3.)
1 What happens to the lines of latitude and longitude at the South and North Poles? Use a globe to help. Can you look East or West from either Pole?
2 Find out one fact about each of these people: Admiral Byrd, Henry Hudson, Ernest Shackleton.

Meeting agendas

Read about agendas and answer the questions.

Meetings are important because they give people an opportunity to meet together to discuss matters of mutual interest or importance. Formal meetings have procedures that allow everyone at the meeting to have a chance to talk about each matter under discussion or to contribute to the meeting.

An important person at the meeting is the chairperson, who must run the meeting according to the rules of conduct of meetings so that all present are involved if they wish to be.

Formal meetings must have an agenda. The agenda is a list of activities or items for discussion, and meeting agendas are the same everywhere. The chairperson develops the agenda with the secretary, and the agenda is made available for everyone to see before the meeting.

The agenda allows continuing items of business to be discussed in the sessions called "Business Arising," and if any new matters arise, the chairperson can refer them to "General Business" for more detailed discussion. The open part of the meeting occurs at General Business, and in the session for Other Business, new matters can be raised by any member.

Formal meetings are an important part of a democratic society. All members present at the meeting can speak, but must also be aware of their responsibilities to speak properly and fairly about any matter or any person.

Here is an example of an agenda.

AGENDA
for the 53rd Meeting of The Hornibrook Bridge Anglers' Club
Date: Tuesday, May 23rd, 2005
Time: 7:30 p.m.
Place: R.S.L. Club, Sandgate
Items
1   Meeting Opening
2   Apologies
3   Minutes of the 52nd Meeting
4   Business Arising from the Minutes
5   Correspondence Inwards/Correspondence Outwards
6   Business Arising from the Correspondence
7   Treasurer's Report
8   President's Report
9   Other Reports
10 General Business (Items are listed.)
11 Other Business
12 Meeting Closure (Set date for next meeting.)

1 Who prepares the agenda for a meeting?

_____

2 Where on the agenda can anyone raise any matter for discussion?

_____

3 What would be included in the Treasurer's Report?

_____

4 What is the name for a record of the meeting kept by the secretary?

_____

5 What does the term "business arising" mean?

_____

6 What is the purpose of "apologies"?

_____

_____

Grammar

Subject groups

A subject group is a group of words that function together with the main noun before or after the verb in a clause. A subject group may be a few words or many words in length.

1 Underline the subject groups in the sentences.

   a) Small, flop-eared dogs make good pets. (two subject groups)

   b) Small, flop-eared dogs with a black patch around one eye make good pets for many people who live in small houses.

2 Increase the number of words in the subject groups. The subject groups are underlined. The first one is done for you. Discuss your sentences with your teacher.

   a) <u>A black cat is unlucky.</u> → A black cat that has four white socks on its paws is unlucky.

   b) <u>Good rain</u> helps the plants grow.

_____

   c) <u>Fast cars</u> are a serious problem.

_____

Punctuation

Set out the agenda for the 3078th annual meeting of the Cilician Horological Society to be held at the School of Arts on Smith Street Georgetown at 7:30 p.m. on Friday December 4, 2005. Use the model provided at the beginning of this unit as a guide.

AGENDA, business arising, general business, apologies, correspondence, Treasurer's Report, minutes, opening, President's Report, other business, closure.

Items: charting the stars, computers and horology, coping with complaints, pricing, disposal of tea bags, cards, handlines.
(Place some of these items in Business Arising and some in General Business.)

Word knowledge

Learn these words. Look, say, cover, write and check. Repeat until the word is spelled correctly.

cancelled   convenient   disastrous   echoing   expense   February
friend   gnaw   heroes   jewellery knuckle   replies

1 Write the words in your spelling list and test yourself.
2 Write the words in sentences.

Write the correct form of the words in brackets.

1 The famous actor _____ (cancel) all his appointments after a

_____ (disaster) performance.

2 My friend bought some very _____ (expense) _____ (jewel).

3 The five _____ (hero) _____ (reply) to the special invitation.

Over to you

(You may want to review the "Writing Process" on page 3.)
1 With your school principal's permission, contact the chair of your school's Parents' Council. Ask to see the chair about the preparation of a meeting agenda, and about the way minutes are kept. Make your contact by letter.
2 Obtain a copy of Notice of Meeting and Agenda of a public company. You can get these from any person who has shares in a public company. Study the organization of the agenda. Notice the different items of business.

Magnets

Read about magnets and match the information.

A magnet is an object that will attract other materials made of iron. The word magnet comes from Magnesia, a place in Thessaly in northern Greece, where stones composed of an iron ore called magnetite were found in ancient times. Magnetite is a naturally occurring magnet.

It was later discovered that if a piece of magnetite was hung by a thread or floated on a piece of wood, it would always turn to point north and south. Sailors were quick to use this discovery to help them in their journeys. Clouds tend to make navigation by the sun and stars particularly difficult.

Any object that shows magnetic properties is called a magnet. The invisible force that attracts objects to the magnet is called magnetism. Every magnet has two poles where most of its strength is found. These are called the north pole and the south pole. When it is suspended, a magnet orients itself along a north-south axis or line.

Magnets can be made by stroking a piece of metal such as a strong needle with another magnet, thus magnetizing the needle.

A remarkable property of magnets is that, when broken, a north pole will appear on one of the broken ends and a south pole on the other. Each piece has its own north and south poles. This polarity allows magnets to establish a magnetic field, a principle that is applied and widely used in many modern appliances, and in any process requiring electromagnetism.

Match the words in Column A to their explanations in Column B.

Column A	Column B
1 magnetite	a caused by magnetic polarity
2 Magnesia	b an area of Thessaly
3 sun and stars	c useful for making magnets
4 magnetic poles	d application of electromagnetism
5 magnetic field	e "floating" magnetite
6 Thessaly	f a natural magnet
7 steel and iron	g barriers to celestial navigation
8 finding North	h used in celestial navigation
9 clouds	i a province in northern Greece
10 microwave	j north and south poles of magnets

Grammar

Infinitive form of the verb

The infinitive form of a verb is shown with the use of the word **to** in front of the verb.
Example to run, to seek, to hide, to find, to have, to be

Underline the infinitives. The first is done for you.

1 Tom wanted <u>to run</u> his winning race again.

2 Sarah went to visit her grandmother.

3 Giuseppe tried to talk quietly.

4 Wanting to go to the movies, Bill and Joan worked hard at home to increase their pocket money. (Clue: only two infinitives.)

5 Alice was too excited to sleep properly.

6 Lewis tried to get his pony to jump the creek.

Verb forms

Complete the following table.

infinitive	present participle	past participle
to run	running	ran
to capture		
		taught
	exercising	
		skid
	being	
		had
to grow		
		sunk
	going	

Splitting the infinitive

Consider the following sentences.
1 Giuseppe quickly tried to talk.
2 Giuseppe tried to talk quickly.
3 Giuseppe tried to quickly talk.

The adverb **quickly** has been used to show how Giuseppe tried to talk, and placing **quickly** at different points in the sentence changes the meaning of the sentence. The meaning of the first two sentences is clear, Giuseppe tried quickly to talk or he talked quickly. In the third sentence, **quickly** has been used to split the infinitive **to talk**. Although it might mean the same as sentence 2, it is not as clear.

As a general rule, it is not useful to split the infinitive by putting other words between **to** and the verb. Only split the infinitive if you think that placing another word in the middle will help your sentence to say exactly what you wish it to say.

Where would you put the adverbs (in brackets)? The infinitives are underlined for you.

1 The children rushed to the table <u>to eat</u>. (greedily, noisily)

   _____

   _____

2 The horses in the distance appeared <u>to float</u> above the ground. (magically)

   _____

   _____

3 We had stopped <u>to check</u> the water in the radiator when Jennifer became ill. (only)

   _____

   _____

4 Pushing <u>to be</u> the first person in the line can lead to an accident. (dangerously)

   _____

   _____

Word knowledge

Learn these words. Look, say, cover, write and check. Repeat until the word is spelled correctly.

volcano	benefited	solid	liquid
continued	included	approached	appeal
appointed	contestant	basin	applied

1 Write the words in your spelling list and test yourself.
2 Write the words in sentences.

Write the correct form of the words in brackets.

1 The two _____ (volcano) _____ (continue) to erupt.

2 As we _____ (approach) the author, we produced our books for signing.

3 The host _____ (appeal) to the three _____ (contestant)

to have their names _____ (include) for the major prize.

Over to you

(You may want to review the "Writing Process" on page 3.)

1 Magnets come in a variety of shapes. There are cylindrical magnets used in solenoids in electromagnetic applications. Have you used bar magnets and horseshoe magnets in classroom experiments to show magnetic fields? You place a sheet of paper over the magnet and sprinkle iron filings on the paper. You will reveal some of the hidden patterns in nature. Write a short report on magnetic fields using the following headings: what they are, where and why they exist, and how they are useful.

2 What are gimbals? Why are they so important? How accurate would magnets have been in rough weather at sea before the invention of the gimbals?

From the Yukon Region to Australia

Read the report and answer the questions.

Each August, whimbrels start arriving in large flocks, having flown thousands of kilometres from the far north of the northern hemisphere to Australia, with the islands of Indonesia as a stopover. The birds disperse from Western Australia to the east coast of Australia.

Whimbrels are among the world's greatest voyagers. Every northern autumn, these curved-beak waders leave on epic flights, often across thousands of kilometres of open ocean. Whimbrels breed in the northern summer in the Yukon region of Alaska and in the Ural Mountains of Russia. These migratory birds fatten up in the northern summer in preparation for their flight to Australia.

In the rich muddy estuaries of northern Queensland, ornithologists wait to record the arrival of the whimbrels. Many whimbrels roost at sites at the mouth of the Barron River in North Queensland. From here they have been observed to fly twenty kilometres out to sea to find crustaceans. Usually thought to be a coastal bird, whimbrels have been recorded feeding in the shallows of Lake Broadwater, in Queensland.

Having wintered in the southern summer in Australia, the birds gather again and embark on their long flight to the Yukon and the Urals. It is tantalizing to think how little we know about the wild birds which share our planet. How do these and other migratory birds navigate? Do they follow the sun and stars? Or do they have some ability to align themselves with the Earth's magnetic field?

1 Where do whimbrels go during summer in the northern hemisphere?

_____

2 Give one characteristic of a whimbrel.

_____

3 What do whimbrels eat?

_____

4 Do you find the migration of birds interesting? Write why or why not.

_____

_____

_____

5 Plot the path of the whimbrels from Northern Europe and Asia to Australia.

6 Mark those places where the whimbrels breed in the northern summer, and where they spend the northern winter.

7 Mark the last country they rest in before continuing to Australia.

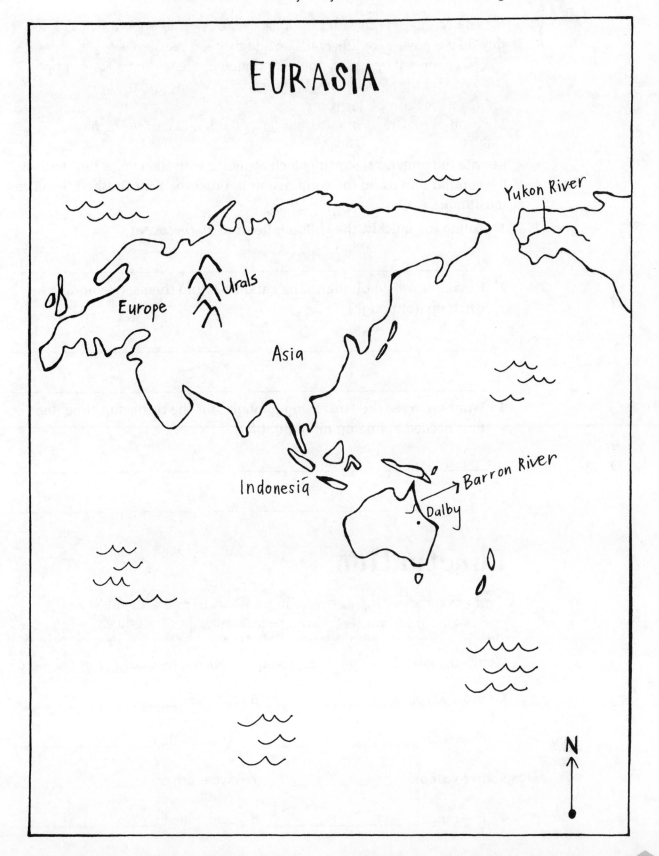

EURASIA

Yukon River

Urals

Europe

Asia

Indonesia

Barron River

Dalby

N

Grammar

Incomplete clauses

Incomplete clauses have an incomplete verb. They are subordinate clauses that do not have a conjunction. Because they are clauses, however, they can be completed by changing their position in the sentence. For example, *Driving down the highway*, my brother took a wrong turn.
This sentence can be rewritten as:
My brother took a wrong turn *(as he was) driving down the highway*.

Rewrite the sentences, starting each sentence with the clause that follows the comma and using the conjunction in brackets. Your finished sentence must make sense.

1   Eating too quickly, the children became ill. (because)

_____

2   Having travelled all night, the children found themselves unable to catch up. (although)

_____

_____

3   Wanting to see the "travelling gimbals" for the thirteenth time, the fans needed to line up all night. (if)

_____

_____

Punctuation

Hyphens are used to join two or more words to make a single expression, as in brother-in-law, walking-stick and forty-five.

Rewrite the following expressions, using a hyphen if necessary, or as one word.

1   peace keeping _____   5   sixty six _____

2   class room _____   6   seven tenths _____

3   five year old _____   7   owner driver _____

4   free range _____   8   hard boiled _____

Word knowledge

SPELL CHECK

Learn these words. Look, say, cover, write and check. Repeat until the word is spelled correctly.

consisted   satisfied   luckily   mainly   obtain   bargain
quaint   complaint   remainder   exclaimed   strait   slippery

1   Write the words in your spelling list and test yourself.
2   Write the words in sentences.

1   Read the word in Column A. Match it up with the word in Column B.

Column A	Column B
get	strange
quaint	contained
fulfil	obtain
consisted	satisfy

2   Write the correct form of the words in brackets.

a)   The shopkeeper was _____ (satisfy) that he had had a

_____ (luck) day.

b)   We _____ (bargain) for the gift which _____ (consist)
of three pieces.

c)   I _____ (complain) that I had fallen on the _____ (slip)
floor.

Over to you

1   The Indigo Bunting migrates from southeastern Canada to southern
Mexico, the West Indies, and even as far as northern South America,
which is about 3200 km away. Write a report, including a map,
showing the places where this bird spends its life.
2   Peterson's Field Guides are particularly useful for bird identification.
Use this or a similar book as a guide to identifying the birds found at
a particular time in your neighbourhood. Make a class chart of the
birds found around the area of your school.

Assembling a scooter

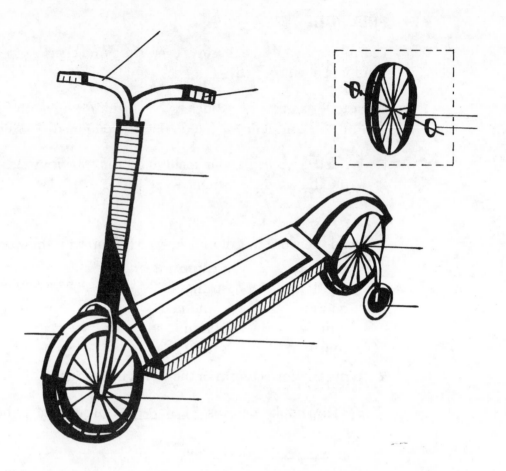

Look at the diagram of a scooter. Match the component names with the line pointing to that part of the scooter, and then reorder the directions below so that you could assemble the scooter for your young brother, sister, cousin or friend.

_____ Place footboard on the ground. Attach frontboard of scooter to the footboard.

_____ Put main wheels onto axles. Secure axles with split pins (total 4).

_____ Attach front guards to frontboard and footboard.

_____ Insert front axle and rear axle.

_____ Attach handles to the top of the frontboard. Put on rubber grips.

_____ Screw locking nuts onto axles.

_____ Assemble and attach trainer wheels (if required).

Grammar

The imperative mood

Directions must be given clearly, and without unnecessary words.

Rewrite the sentences using the verb in the imperative mood. (Hint: Put the underlined verb at the beginning of your new sentence.)

1 To deliver this box, you need to <u>drive</u> as far as the first traffic lights.

_____

2 Creek Street is where you <u>turn</u> right.

_____

3 There is a bus seat on the left and this is where you <u>leave</u> the box.

_____

Sentence completion

Rewrite the sentences so that they make sense. (**Hint**: Move the incomplete clause to the end of the sentence using the conjunction provided. You may need to use words that have been left out in the original sentence.)

Example   Having been told to clean up her room, the trash can was soon filled. (after) → The trash can was soon filled after she had been told to clean up her room.

1 Exploring the mountains for a new road, the horses could not be

taken up the cliffs. (when) _____

_____

2 Wanting to win the Best Pet Contest, the man entered his chihuahua.

(because) _____

_____

3 Going down the road at five in the morning, the sun was peeping over

the mountain. (as) _____

_____

Punctuation

Rewrite the following text as a list of instructions, using bullets for each line. Start each line with a verb in the imperative mood and place any extra information in brackets. The first two lines have been done for you.

You put one tablespoon each of green and black peppercorns which are cracked into a bowl, then pour in one cup of olive oil, stir in half of a cup of French dressing or vinegar and herbs mixture, add two tbsp dill, dried or freshly chopped, squeeze two cloves of garlic and mix in quarter of a cup of lime juice. A half-cup of white cooking wine is added, together with one hot chili with seeds removed. The mixture is thoroughly shaken and stirred. This marinade can be used for seafood such as shrimp or squid.

- Put green and black peppercorns (cracked) in a bowl.
- Pour in one cup olive oil.

_____

_____

_____

_____

_____

_____

Word knowledge

SPELL CHECK

Learn these words. Look, say, cover, write and check. Repeat until the word is spelled correctly.

describe	satisfied	practise	exercise	honour	armour
favourite	encourage	surfaced	curved	suburbs	urged

Note: **practise** is a verb.
1 Write the words in your spelling list and test yourself.
2 Write the words in sentences.

Write the correct form of the words in brackets.

1 They _____ (exercise) and _____ (practise) in an attempt to be chosen for the team.

2 The tour guide _____ (describe) the _____ (curve)

    _____ (surface) of the building.

3 Our friends _____ (encourage) us to be _____ (satisfy) with our result.

Over to you

(You may want to review the "Writing Process" on page 3.)

1 Survey the students in your class to find out how many households have electrical appliances such as VCRs, DVD players, microwaves, and so on. Ask each student if they know how to use the appliances and how well they can use them. Record your findings in a table.

		Use:		
Appliance	Number	well	a little	cannot use

2 Which appliance do they know least about? Write a procedure for using that appliance in some way.

Letters seeking and giving information

1 Read this letter from Ryan seeking information. It is written as a formal letter:

March 31, 2005
Mr. Harry Smythe
Manager
Forest Park
London, ON
L3M 7A5

Dear Mr. Smythe:

Re: Fitness Trail Forest Park

I am nine years old. Every day I go with my parents along the Fitness Trail at Forest Park. My parents are able to use the fitness stations to exercise but the stations are too far off the ground for me to use.

I was wondering if it would be possible for the park authority to put in a junior fitness trail for children about my age (nine years old), next to the existing fitness trail. I have some good ideas if you would like to hear them.

Yours sincerely,
Ryan McKnight

36 Wheeler Drive
London, ON
K4N 7B5

Remember

In formal letters:
- commas are used in addresses, but periods are **not**
- proper punctuation is used in each paragraph
- a colon is used after the greeting or salutation, e.g. **Dear Sir: Dear Sir/Madam:** With these, use a formal closure, **Yours faithfully**.
- when using **Dear Mr. James:** or **Dear Ms. Carter:** use the closure, **Yours sincerely**
- **Re**: may be used to tell in a phrase what the letter is about
- use a paragraph for each idea.

1 Answer these questions.

a) Who wrote the letter?

_____

b) What is the problem with the fitness station?

_____

c) Who is Mr. Smythe?

_____

d) What fitness stations do you think Ryan would suggest?

_____

2 Write Mr. Smythe's reply to Ryan McKnight.

Date

Name and address of person to whom you are writing

_____

_____

_____

Dear _____

Re: _____

Use one paragraph for each idea. Write at least three paragraphs.

_____

_____

_____

_____

_____

_____

_____

Yours (sincerely or faithfully) depending on name or position/title used.

Your name and address

P.S. Don't forget to sign the letter.

Grammar

Subject–verb agreement

A singular subject is followed by a singular verb when it is introduced by phrases beginning with: **with**, **like** and **as well as**.

1 Rewrite each sentence with different nouns as subjects. (The nouns are in **bold** in the first sentence.)

a) The **girl**, with her **friend**, was late for **class**.

_____

b) Tom, like Harry, is tall for his age.

_____

c) Jenny, as well as Ari, rides to school.

_____

d) The boy, with his dog, is having a swim.

_____

2 Complete the sentences. Remember to use a singular verb.

a) The horse, with a pony, _____.

b) The Empire State Building, like the United Nations building,

_____.

c) David, as well as Aisha, _____.

d) The team, with the coach, _____.

Punctuation

Statements always end in a period.
Example This is tomato soup.
Questions ask for an answer and have a question mark.
Example Is this tomato soup?
An exclamation exclaims something and has an exclamation mark.
Example I've won first prize!

Say whether each sentence is a statement, question or exclamation, and add the correct punctuation at the end. There is one of each.

1 A week has 7 days _____

2 How cold it is today _____

3 Is it going to rain tomorrow _____

Word knowledge

SPELL CHECK

Learn these words. Look, say, cover, write and check. Repeat until the word is spelled correctly.

ordinary   primary   regular   popular   particular   pleasant
assistant   vacant   instance   importance   ambulance   entrance

1 Write the words in your spelling list and test yourself.
2 Write the words in sentences.

Over to you

(You may want to review the "Writing Process" on page 3.)
1 Write a letter to a person from history whom you admire, such as Martin Luther King or Florence Nightingale, asking a question you would like answered.
2 Why or why not would you like to deliver mail to other planets?

Visual language

1 Read this extract.

Stratosphere

The Earth's atmosphere has three layers of air extending upwards into the sky. The first layer above the Earth is the troposphere which extends between 10 km and 19 km upwards from the Earth's surface. The temperature falls with increasing height. In the troposphere, cumulus clouds (fluffy with a flat base) form.

The layer of atmosphere above the troposphere is the stratosphere where the density of the air is thin and there is little change in temperature. In the lower stratosphere, cirrus clouds (like mare's tails) form. This is a region of turbulent jet "trade winds" of 80–160 km an hour.

Higher in the stratosphere, the temperature is increased by the action of the sun's ultraviolet rays on the ozone (a condensed form of oxygen) that accumulates there. It is this ozone layer which absorbs the ultraviolet rays from the sun and protects the Earth from excessive ultraviolet radiation. Above the stratosphere is the ionosphere, a region of electrical activity in which radio waves are reflected. The ionosphere is used to make long-distance phone and radio transmissions around the world.

2 Draw a diagram showing the four regions in the extract. Show important information about each region. Write the names of the four regions along the left hand horizontal side. Start with the troposphere at the bottom of the diagram.

Posters

Design a poster using all the information from the paragraph below.

It was a two-roomed house built of rough timber. A veranda with four posts went across the front of the house. The front door was a faded red. At the back of the house, a kitchen built of the same material was visible. The three chimneys had a slight lean to them. Smoke was drifting lazily from the kitchen chimney. A small child was playing under a large maple tree near the gate to the field.

Term 3

Letter writing

Write an informal note to thank a neighbour or friend who has done you a great favour, such as minded your pet or given you a lift.

Tips
- Express your thanks simply and with sincerity.
- Be straightforward and brief.

Date _____

Dear _____

Write a paragraph or three sentences.

_____

_____

_____

_____

_____

Closure _____

Signed

Procedure

The correct way of turning a computer on depends on the type of computer you have.

For a personal computer, press the Power On button which is usually found on the CPU tower.

If your computer has an external hard disk drive, switch the disk drive on first.

If you have a laptop computer, press any key on the keyboard (except caps lock) to wake your computer.

For a palm pilot, use the stylus (a small pointed tool) to press the ON button.

Illustrate how to switch on the different types of computers. Write a caption under each illustration.

Explanation

Read this extract. Note six points in your own words.

Fruit or vegetable?

In 1893, in an attempt to clarify the difference between what is a fruit and what is a vegetable, the United States Supreme Court said that vegetables were eaten as part of a main course of a meal. Fruit was said to be eaten as a dessert, or a snack, or as an appetizer.

Is such a difference correct according to a dictionary or how people use fruit and vegetables in everyday life?

Tomatoes, sweet corn, eggplant, avocado and Jerusalem artichoke are eaten as part of the main course of a meal, but does that make them vegetables?

In botany (the study of plants), a fruit is the ripened ovary (where the seeds are kept) of a plant. A tomato is a fruit and an avocado is a fruit or a vegetable.

If we go into a fruit store to buy fruit we would buy juicy-type fruit such as apples, oranges, mandarins, pineapples, grapes, watermelon and other melons.

Vegetables in everyday life include potatoes, carrots, beets, zucchinis, squash, lettuce and cabbage.

_____

_____

_____

_____

_____

_____

Narrative

Read the text and answer the questions.

Wayne Gretzky: No. 99

Wayne Gretzky was born in Brantford, Ontario on January 26, 1961, the eldest of five children. Hockey was part of his life from the beginning. At age 2, he received his first pair of skates and, with a cut-down hockey stick, made his first appearance on the ice.

At age 6, he skated with ten-year-olds. By age 10, he scored 378 goals in one season of 82 games. Even at this young age, there was talk that he might be as great as his hockey hero Gordie Howe.

At age 17, Wayne began his professional career in 1978 with the Indianapolis Racers of the World Hockey Association.

In the same year he was traded to the Edmonton Oilers of the National Hockey League (the NHL). Gretzky, the Great One as he came to be known, led the Oilers to four Stanley Cups over the next ten years.

In 1988, Gretzky married Janet Jones. They have three children.

In 1989 he was traded to the Los Angeles Kings for two players, three first-round choices and $15 million dollars. On October 15, 1989, No.99 became the No.1 all-time NHL scorer with his 1851st point. He surpassed his long-time hero, Gordie Howe, another hockey legend.

Wayne Gretzky led the league in scoring nine times from 1981 to 1987 and in 1990 and 1991. He was also named the NHL's most valuable player from 1979 to 1987.

At the end of the 1995 season, he was traded to the St. Louis Blues but was soon traded to the New York Rangers. He played for the Rangers until his retirement in 1999. Out of respect for this superb hockey player, his hockey shirt, number 99, was hung up forever when he retired. He is still considered the greatest hockey player of all time.

1 Who was Gretzky's hockey idol? _____

2 State two examples of how, even at an early age, Gretzky was clearly a talented hockey player.

_____

3 How does hanging up Gretzky's hockey shirt (No. 99) show respect for him?

_____

4 What are some of the reasons hockey players are traded? Which of these reasons do you think applied to Wayne Gretzky when he was traded?

_____

_____

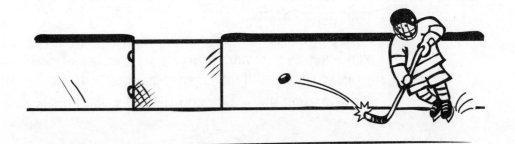

Leiningen Versus the Ants

(A retelling of the story by Carl Stephenson)

Deep in the Brazilian jungle, an agitated District Commissioner warned Leiningen of the approach of twenty square miles of ants. Confidently, he said he would use his intelligence against the ants. The 400 people who worked for Leiningen believed in him. After all, Leiningen had made ample preparations.

He had built a twelve-foot wide, horseshoe-shaped water ditch around the plantation, meeting the river at both ends. The weir could further flood the ditch. He also had built an inner moat around the hill on which his house stood.

Once his men sighted the ants, he left his hammock, mounted his horse and rode leisurely south to see a two-mile wide line of ants approaching quickly in perfect formation.

After the eastern and western flanks found no way through the moat, the ants were soon using their fellow fallen ants as stepping stones to get across the southern ditch. Surprised by their quick advance, Leiningen ordered the river to be dammed further. The rising ditch water level slowed the ants' progress so much that the workers rejoiced. Confident, Leiningen slept well that night.

The ants remained quiet on the southern ditch. However, to the west, they had gnawed stems off tamarind leaves for other ants to carry to the ditch to use as rafts to cross the ditch. Leiningen realized he had underestimated his opponents.

So, he ordered the ditch water to be substantially decreased. They waited before flooding the water. This method temporarily slowed the ants' progress.

Leiningen retreated to the inner moat and filled the ditch with oil. Again confident, he slept well only to awake to discover that for several hours the ants had been filling the oil ditch with twigs and bark to use as a sidewalk to walk across the oil in the ditch.

Leiningen lit the oil ditch on fire. As soon as the flames died out, the remaining ants began to rebuild their "sidewalk." This process took less time than before as the oil surface was covered in ashes from the fire. Leiningen had more oil put in the ditch and the ditch re-lit. This process was repeated three times before he realized that the ants were eventually going to get across.

In a last desperate act, Leiningen raced to the weir to flood his whole plantation. Even though he wore goggles, heavy gloves, and covered himself in oil, some ants still managed to get inside his clothes and bite him.

He reached the wheel and turned it several times, flooding the

plantation. As he ran back, he felt the ants all over his body. He nearly stumbled—a sure death—but refused to lose to the ants. He reached home. The workers told him all the ants were carried away by the great sweeping water. Leiningen grinned and fell asleep.

1   Who are the characters in the story?

_____

2   Describe the setting in your own words.

_____

_____

3   What two characteristics do Leiningen and the ants share?

_____

4   Describe the cleverest strategy belonging to either Leiningen or the ants.

_____

_____

Grammar

Subject–verb agreement

Find the clause subject of a sentence by asking who is doing what, or what is doing what.

Example	Leiningen	ran to the weir.
	Who is involved? (subject)	What is he doing? (verb)
	Ants	chewed the stems off tamarind leaves.
	What is involved? (subject)	What are they doing? (verb)

Underline the subjects and circle the verbs in these simple sentences.

1   The old man walks down the road in the morning.

2   Heavy trucks race along the highway.

3   At school, children enjoy their lunch hour.

4   Sarah likes ice cream, too.

5   The dog watched for the rabbit all night.

Sentence completion

Use the correct form of the verbs and adjectives in brackets to complete the sentences.

1   In many places, the Brazilian jungle _____ (consist) of lush

vegetation _____ and _____ (dense) undergrowth.

2   Some examples _____ (is) the tamarind and bamboo.

3   The trees _____ (grow) much _____ (tall) in the forests

and rain forests of the _____ (wet) coastal lands and mountains.

4   Dogs _____ (is) _____ (valuable) to farmers than cats,

and they _____ (must) be the _____ (brave)

of animals.

Punctuation

Commas are also used to mark off information that tells you more about something in the sentence.

Place commas in the correct positions. The first is done for you.

1   We visited the old homestead, a solid home for generations of farmers, on the weekend.

2   The old part of the house which still had a wood floor was attached to the rear of the living room.

3   Sara gave her friend Wilson who had played on her soccer team since Grade 3 a soccer ball as a birthday present.

4   The breed of a dog and every farmer had to have a dog or two was less important than its bravery and loyalty.

Word knowledge

Learn these words. Look, say, over, write and check. Repeat until the word is spelled correctly.

weir	traverse	voracious	agitated	confident	approaching
moat	tamarind	hammock	invincible	swathed	concrete

1 Write the words in your spelling list and test yourself.
2 Write the words in sentences.

1 Replace the word or phrase in *italics* with a word from the Spell Check.

   a) In medieval times, *water-filled ditches*_____ surrounded castles for security

   b) He was so hungry, he ate *quickly* _____ly at dinner.

   c) The hare was too *self-assured* _____ and that's why he lost the race to the tortoise.

   d) The *wheel* _____ controls the flow of water from the river.

2 Circle the word that doesn't fit in each list.

   a) finish, end, begin, complete

   b) imprison, release, liberate

   c) purchase, buy, sell, acquire

Over to you

(You may want to review the "Writing Process" on page 3.)
1 Describe a time when you had to confront a really difficult situation. Explain what was difficult about it.
2 Describe two strategies you used to be successful in that situation. Describe at least one more strategy you now realize you could have used to be successful.

Speeches: Introducing a guest speaker

1 How do you introduce a guest speaker to your class? Think about the following questions. You might even like to talk about these questions with some members of your class.

- Who introduces the speaker?
- What do you say?
- For how long do you talk?
- What information do you give about the speaker?
- Who is the speaker?
- From where does she/he come?
- What is useful background information?
- Do you say anything about the speech?
- Do you thank the speaker? If not, who does and how?
- How do you welcome the speaker?

2 Now compare your notes with these below.

The time has come for the guest speaker to address the meeting. The chairperson, or the person given the task of introducing the speaker, stands up and calls for everyone's attention by saying something like "I now call this meeting to order for the purpose of listening to our visitor." This is usually enough for most people to stop talking and listen to the introduction.

The chairperson welcomes all the members and any other guests at the meeting, then turns to and welcomes the speaker. The introduction includes the following information.

- Welcome to members and guests
- Welcome to guest speaker, clearly stating title and name
- Statement about the speaker's background: occupation, any outstanding things the speaker has done like other speeches, published books, activities, etc.
- Statement of the title of the speech
- Very brief statement of the purpose of the invitation (why the speaker was invited to address the members)
- Restatement of the speaker's name and the title of the speech. For example, "Please welcome our guest speaker this afternoon, Dr. Tina McJacobsen, who will tell us about her work in organizing civil defence organizations in the event of natural disasters." The chairperson then begins clapping and leads the clapping until the speaker is standing and ready to begin to speak.

Grammar

Subordinate clauses

Subordinate clauses cannot make sense on their own, and must be used with a subordinate clause. For example, "If I go to town tomorrow" is not a complete sentence. This conditional "if" clause needs to be matched with an independent clause in a complex sentence such as "I will buy a new pair of shoes if I go to town tomorrow."

Match the subordinate clauses with an appropriate independent clause. Make sure that you use the correct punctuation, using capital letters at the beginning of the sentence and a period at the end. If the subordinate clause is used at the beginning of the sentence, use a comma between it and the following independent clause.

Subordinate clauses	Independent clauses
1 because he had no money left	a Mr. Patel would read the main stories each morning
2 while the driver waited	b the navigator worked quickly with maps and compass
3 unless she had something better to do	c Phillip enjoyed the latest movies
4 if the newspaper was delivered early	d Sasha went to the movies for the day
5 since she came to the West Coast	e Jonathon was forced to walk home that evening
6 when he had the time to go	f Gina has been sending cards to her friends at home

1 _____

2 _____

3 _____

4 _____

5 _____

6 _____

Sentence construction

A loose sentence is one where the independent clause appears first in the sentence.

Example   <u>He joined the Air Force</u>   <u>because he had always loved flying</u>.
                        ↑   ↑
               independent clause   subordinate clause

In a periodic sentence, the subordinate clause appears first.

Example   <u>Because she loved jet engines,</u>   <u>she joined the navy</u>.
                        ↑   ↑
               subordinate clause   independent clause

(Note the use of the comma after the subordinate clause in a periodic sentence.)

1 Complete these periodic sentences. Remember the comma.

    a) However hard Billy tried _____.

    b) Whenever the girls wanted nachos _____.

    c) If that task is not completed on time _____.

    d) Whether he wanted to or not _____.

    e) Because he wanted to help people _____.

2 Complete these loose sentences. Underline the conjunction you use for your subordinate clause. (Choose conjunctions from the box.)

because when if since although where since however until unless

    a) The chihuahua kept falling over _____.

    b) The pelicans kept coming to us _____.

    c) Grandad was called Opa only _____.

    d) He had tried his best to walk 300 kilometres _____.

    e) Her magic became more entrancing _____.

Word knowledge

SPELL CHECK

Learn these words. Look, say, cover, write and check. Repeat until the word is spelled correctly.

athletics	awkward	balcony	besiege
casualty	crystal	desperate	disease
forehead	frontier	holiday	hurriedly

1 Write the words in your spelling list and test yourself.
2 Write the words in sentences.

1 Replace the word or phrase in *italics* with a word from the Spell Check. (Remember to use the correct form of the word.)

    a) The city walls were *attacked* _____ by armed soldiers.

    b) We left the football game *in a great hurry* _____.

    c) She threw the ball *ungracefully* _____.

    d) The weather ruined the *vacation* _____.

2 Circle the odd word out in each list.

    a) top, height, summit, bottom

    b) feel, touch, sniff, shake

    c) examine, wear, inspect, look

Over to you

(You may want to review the "Writing Process" on page 3.)
1 Call a class meeting and decide whom you would like to invite to speak to the class. With your teacher's approval, send a letter of invitation. Select a meeting chairperson and a person to move a vote of thanks. In groups, work out the introduction and the vote of thanks.
2 Find out about the following terms: standing orders, gag, point of order, chairperson's ruling, Hansard.

What makes an electric bell ring?

Read the text and answer the questions.

What makes an electric bell work? No one knows exactly what electricity is, but we know that it can do many useful things. Who does not know that when an electric bell is pushed it will ring for as long as the button is pressed?

It is known that electricity is conducted by certain materials. One material along which it flows like a current is copper wire. Two separate copper wires are connected to the bell button.

At one end of the wires is an ordinary door bell fixed with a tiny hammer mounted on a spring, and a device known as a contact breaker. Connected to one of the wires is an electric battery.

The two wires are placed so that their ends do not meet each other. A bell button of a non-conducting material, such as plastic, is used. When a doorbell button is pressed, the two pieces of wire are connected and instantly electrical energy from the battery leaps along the wire. This energy races from behind the bell button towards the bell. When it reaches the hammer of the bell, it finds the way blocked (impeded) and sets up a disturbance which causes the hammer to strike the bell.

A single ring from a bell would not be always heard and that would not make it useful. To overcome the problem a rapid ringing is given out by the bell. Electrical energy is lost each time a bell is rung. As a bell is designed to work for a short period, the battery seldom dies immediately, as it has time to recover.

1   List five appliances that are powered by electricity.

_____

2   What metal wire is used most widely as an electrical conductor?

_____

3   What happens when a bell's button or switch is pushed?

_____

_____

4   What other devices do people put on their doors to make a noise?

_____

Grammar

Relative clauses

A relative clause gives more information about someone or something, and usually begins with one of these words: **who**, **which**, **that**, **whose**, **whom**. (In special instances, other words such as **when** and **where** can introduce a relative clause.)

Example This is the house **that** Jack built.

This is the dog **that** chased the boy **who** lives with his parents **whose** house was built by Jack.

Read these sentences. Underline the relative clauses, and circle the word that it is telling more about (that it relates to). There is at least one relative clause in each sentence.

1 Electricity is the energy that makes an electric bell work.

2 The electrical appliances that I have in my bedroom are a CD and a walkman.

3 The person whom we call to fix the electrical wires is the electrician.

4 The current finds its way blocked and sets up a disturbance, which causes the hammer to strike the bell.

5 The children whose electric bells sounded the best were given a certificate.

door bell

CD player

walkman

electrician

Pronouns and their references

Pronouns refer to other words in a text, but they can sometimes refer to more or other words than the writer intended.

Read the sentences and rewrite them to complete or correct their meaning. The problem pronouns are in **bold**.

1 Benjamin went fishing with his daughter Rachel and his son David. **They** said **they** liked it.

(Rewrite to indicate clearly to whom "they" refers—there is more than one answer.)

_____

_____

2 *The Old Man and the Sea* is a famous short novel by Ernest Hemingway. **He** catches a fish which drags **him** across the sea in **his** small boat.

_____

_____

Punctuation

Hyphens can be used to join two nouns. The first word is not meant to be an adjective.
Example owner-driver

Insert hyphens where necessary.

1 She was their first girl child.

2 The woman was ice skating on her backyard pond.

3 The class took part in a cross country race.

4 I joined a new book club in my neighbourhood.

5 He put the keys on the key ring.

Word knowledge

SPELL CHECK

Learn these words. Look, say, cover, write and check. Repeat until the word is spelled correctly.

exported	florist	orphan	uniform	ceased	increased
bungalow	threaten	revealed	retreated	dreary	requested

1 Write the words in your spelling list and test yourself.
2 Write the words in sentences.

1 Replace the word or phrase in *italics* with a word from the Spell Check. Remember to use the correct form of the word.

a) Beautiful bowls of flowers were arranged by the *flower arrangers*

_____ .

b) Many cows were *sent out* _____ to overseas countries.

c) Some soldiers under shellfire *withdrew* _____ to their base.

d) All the players were *asked* _____ to leave.

2 Homonyms are words that sound the same or similar, but are spelled differently and have different meanings. They are frequently confused, causing spelling errors. Look up the meanings of the following pairs of homonyms and use each in a sentence.

weather	through	wear	right	seen
whether	thorough	where	write	scene

Over to you

1 The electricity that we use every day is generated by a variety of sources. What are our sources of electric power?
2 Make a list showing the value that electricity has and the problems it brings.

Film reviews

1 A film review provides particular information about a film. Read the review to find out about the film *Little Women*.

Title: *Little Women*
Actors: Winona Ryder, Susan Sarandon, Christian Bale
Film Classification: G for All ages
Rating: ****
Little Women is based on the 1868 novel by Louisa May Alcott. It tells the story of the four March sisters, Meg, Jo, Beth and Amy in the years of the Civil War period in America. The many adventures of the girls as they grew into adulthood is an important part of the film, which is well acted and beautifully filmed. The story of the family is narrated by Jo.
Reviewer: Asif Korma

2 Write a film review for a film you have seen. Use the format above.

_____

_____

_____

_____

_____

_____

_____

_____

_____

_____

_____

_____

Grammar

Loose and periodic sentences

In a loose sentence, the independent clause appears first in the sentence.
Example
The pool was closed because there were few people using it in winter.
       ↑   ↑

  independent clause   subordinate clause

In a periodic sentence, the subordinate clause comes first.
Example
Because there were few people using it in winter, the pool was closed.
              ↑   ↑

        subordinate clause   independent clause

Note the use of the comma after the subordinate clause when it is placed at the beginning of the sentence.

1 Complete these periodic sentences. (Remember the comma.)

   a) Because it was raining _____.

   b) However she went _____.

   c) Unless there is a full team _____.

   d) If the train is late _____.

   e) Since their last visit _____.

   f) Although he tried hard _____.

2 Complete these loose sentences. Underline the conjunctions used to introduce the subordinate clauses.

   a) He went to the store as soon as _____.

   b) The family has been gone since _____.

   c) I need to know whether _____.

   d) We will wait until _____.

   e) I will send it unless _____.

   f) The party was a tremendous success because _____.

Sentence construction

A text about any topic makes use of words or vocabulary about that topic. For example, it is not usual to use opera terms when describing a local baseball game. Opera would use musical terms and words about tenors, sopranos, divas and codas. Baseball is about pitchers, batters, bases, catches, plays, home runs, pinch hits and so on.

Circle words from the list below that would be appropriate in writing a report about pizza. You may add other words that are appropriate to your report.

pan, base, cheese, mozzarella, tomatoes, ground beef, oboe, drum,

anchovies, euphonium, onion, trombone, paste, brass, plate, band,

master, trumpet, mace, parsley, chives, basil, dill, kettle, snare, salad

_____

Write a paragraph (on a separate sheet) about one of the two topics in this list.

Punctuation

A colon (:) is used in setting out information.
Title:
Actors:
Movie:
Rating:
Reviewer:

Use the format above and fill in details of a movie you have seen.

_____

_____

_____

_____

_____

Word knowledge

SPELL CHECK

Learn these words. Look, say, cover, write and check. Repeat until the word is spelled correctly.

amusement	amazement	instrument	monument
equipment	science	ancient	thief
relief	mischief	shriek	series

1 Write the words in your spelling list and test yourself.
2 Write the words in sentences.

Replace the word or phrase in *italics* with a word from the Spell Check. Remember to use the correct form of the word.

1 The surgeon's *tools* _____ were on the operating table.

2 The girl heard a *loud, sharp, shrill cry* _____ .

3 The scientist placed the *items to carry out the experiment*

_____ on the bench.

4 They found *very old* _____ utensils at the archeological site.

Over to you

(You may want to review the "Writing Process" on page 3.)
1 Go to your Saturday or weekend newspaper and find the movie section. Read the review of a film that you would be interested in seeing. Write your own review of the film from the information provided.
2 From which book would you make a film, and why?

Science experiment

Organisms that cause decay—Mould

Think about what things mould will grow on:

- plastic? _____
- paper? _____
- wood? _____
- butter? _____
- carrots? _____
- metal? _____

Investigation: gathering information (data)

Make a mould terrarium by using a clear container with a tightly-fitting lid.
A large jar works well.
Place a layer of soil or sand in the jar.
Pour in enough water to make soil or sand damp.
Choose items you want to test and place in jar.
Keep a list of all items placed in terrarium (jar).
Keep lid tightly on the jar and place it in a warm place.
List materials on which you believe mould will grow.
Watch for mould growth.
Record date of mould growth.
Empty the terrarium and check what happened to all the items.
Are all the moulds the same shape and colour?

Record keeping

Topic: mould growth

Object	Date put in	Prediction	Result	Date
1 Carrot 2	July 5	Mould	Yes	July 10

Research report

Read this report on the experiment and answer the questions.

Moulds: Why did the items in the jar decompose?

The items we put in the jar had mould spores on them before we put them in. Bread mould was black and cotton-like. It got food from the bread. Some moulds are called parasites. Parasite moulds are found on fruit and vegetables. These moulds cause fruit and vegetables to rot or decompose. Moulds are found in soil and water. The most destructive mould occurs on potatoes.

1 How did the mould get in the jar? _____

_____

2 Describe the mould on bread. _____

3 Tell where parasite moulds can be found. _____

_____

4 Are moulds found in water? _____

5 On what plant does the most destructive mould occur? _____

Experiment: testing for moulds on food

This is an easy experiment. Items that you could use include bread,
cheese, jam, peanut butter, mayonnaise or cream.
Leave the items exposed to the air.
Put a small amount of moisture on each to aid the growth of mould.
Set out the steps of your experiment.
1 Place (each item) in terrarium.
2 Keep list of items placed in terrarium.

_____

_____

_____

_____

_____

_____

_____

_____

Grammar

Participles and gerunds

> The participle form of the verb can be used as a noun.
> *Example* Swimming is not allowed.
> Ask: "What is not allowed?"
> The answer is that something is not allowed, and that something is "swimming." This means that "swimming" is being used as a noun. When the participle form of the verb is used on its own as a noun, it is called a gerund.

Underline the gerunds. Remember the test. The first sentence is done for you.

1 <u>Walking</u> is good exercise.

2 Testing for moulds didn't take long.

3 Adding moisture will help to make the mould grow.

4 We were doing the experiment when Tim broke the jar.

5 We were having trouble describing the moulds.

6 Writing the report was the interesting part.

Sentence construction

Change the tense of the verbs in each sentence from the future tense to the past tense. The verbs are <u>underlined</u>. Be very careful with number 3.
Example The mould <u>will grow</u> on the bread, rice cakes and sponge.
          The mould <u>grew</u> on the bread, rice cakes and sponge.

1 My friends <u>will start</u> their experiment on moulds eagerly.

   _____

2 Abed <u>will be writing</u> up the experiment in its final form.

   _____

3 Everyone <u>will be wondering</u> what <u>happens</u> to the spinach in the jar.

   _____

Word knowledge

SPELL CHECK

Learn these words. Look, say, cover, write and check. Repeat until the word is spelled correctly.

telephone	telescope	celebrated	debt
doubt	forwarding	awarded	traffic
panic	convicted	respectfully	selected

1   Write the words in your spelling list and test yourself.
2   Write the words in sentences.

Replace the word or phrase in *italics* with a word from the Spell Check. Remember to use the correct form of the word.

1   Many astronomers used a *large magnifying glass*

_____ to observe the moon.

2   In the competition the woman was *given* _____ first

prize.

3   For my birthday I *chose* _____ a new pair of jeans.

4   The *instrument that carries voices from other places*

_____ rang.

Over to you

(You may want to review the "Writing Process" on page 3.)
1   Do another research activity or investigation to study the rate of decomposition of different leaves and foods. Follow the model provided in this unit.
2   Why do farmers encourage the growth of moulds in cheese? Find out what the following cheeses have in common, and write a sentence or two about each: Stilton, blue-vein, Gorgonzola, Roquefort.

mouldy cheese . . . .

Letters of complaint and praise

Letters of complaint

Sometimes it is necessary to write a letter of complaint. A simple letter is often able to resolve the matter. Remember that we all make mistakes, so letters of complaint should be polite.

Tips

- Gather all your facts: date, time, what the problem is, what happened, date of purchase, docket/receipt number and so on.
- Use paragraphs to set out your points.
- Keep a copy of your letter.

1 Read this letter.

September 10, 2005
The Manager
K Mart
PO Box 2589
Milton, ON
E1A 3K6

Dear Sir/Madam:

Re: Faulty No Brand Basketball

At the Milton K Mart on September 9, 2005 I bought a No Brand basketball, serial number FLAT2345908. I paid $22.95.
My sister and I played with the ball for about an hour at the local court. We noticed that the ball was not bouncing very well. When we got home my father pumped up the ball but it would not go up. During the night it went flat.

I am very disappointed and would like my money refunded as I do not want to replace it with the same brand.
A photocopy of my receipt is enclosed.
I look forward to hearing from you.

Yours faithfully,

Amanda Gates
21 Stirling Street
Milton, ON
E4B 2K1
(905) 555-4331

2 Write a letter of complaint for one of the following:
- a skateboard that keeps losing its wheels
- a hair dryer that will not work
- a pen that will only write invisible messages.

Remember to include:
- what was bought and its price
- when and where it was bought
- what the problem is
- what you want done
- a polite finish.

_____

Letters of praise

Tips
- Keep them brief.
- Tell what happened, when and where.
- Tell whom you want thanked.

Grammar

Subject–verb agreement

In any sentence, the subject and verb must agree.
A singular subject has a singular verb. Singular means one.
Example The ball bounced.   Only one ball
          The cat meowed.   Only one cat

Plural means more than one.
Example The balls bounced.   The cats meowed.
          We do not know how many balls or cats but we know there
          are more than one.

1 Complete the sentences, but first check whether the subject is singular
   or plural. Ask yourself how many are involved.

   a) The train _____.

   b) Many women _____.

   c) Outside the station, the travellers _____.

   d) Some players _____.

2 Check these sentences. Is the verb correct (singular/plural) in each
   one? If not, correct the verb.

   a) The man was late for work. _____

   b) Children was on the road. _____

   c) My brother were sick. _____

   d) Accidents is common at that corner. _____

   e) The books are on the shelf. _____

Word knowledge

SPELL CHECK

Learn these words. Look, say, cover, write and check. Repeat until the word is spelled correctly.

advantage	disgrace	disgraceful	dismiss
distress	discovered	display	disturbed
disgusted	disobey	disappeared	disappointed

1 Write the words in your spelling list and test yourself.
2 Write the words in sentences.

An anagram is made by moving the letters of one word to make another word.
Example **reap** becomes **pear**
Read the clues to change each word in bold into an anagram.
The starting letter is given for each anagram.

ride	with great fear or suffering	d _____
time	something very small	m _____
same	found on clothes	s _____
save	a receptacle for flowers	v _____

Over to you

(You may want to review the "Writing Process" on page 3.)
1 Write a letter to your local newspaper telling some of the good things that happen at your school. Ask that your letter be published.
2 Write a letter to your newspaper complaining about your newspaper regularly being delivered to the wrong house.

Visual language

Design your own pictorial signs

Design pictorial signs for the following:
- keep dirty fingers off the windows
- no parking for bikes
- scenic spot to take a photograph.

Teeth

Read this passage, then draw a tooth and label it with information from the text.

There are three parts to a tooth: root, neck and crown. The crown has an outer coating of hard enamel which covers the dentine, the bony framework of the tooth.

A human mouth has 32 teeth. Teeth are able to cut, tear, and grind food.

In each human jaw there are four incisors for biting, four bicuspids for chewing, two canines for holding or tearing, and six molars for grinding.

Wisdom teeth are molars which help the grinding and chewing of food. Wisdom teeth do not usually appear until a person is over 18 years of age.

How to assemble a table

Mr. Wheybridge wanted to put his new table together but found that the dog had torn the instructions. Help him to put the instructions below in the right order, and also match the text to the picture. The first one has been done for you.

  _1_   Untie all pieces, being very careful to place the screws and plates where they will not be lost.

_____ Turn pole upside-down, and position the arms on the round table top. Ensure the holes in the arms match the holes in the bottom of the table top.

_____ Take the centre post A. Attach feet B and C, using plate Y and four screws. Put the screws into the holes prepared for them.

_____ Use screws from bag G to screw the arms to the table top. Tighten all screws firmly but not too hard.

_____ Fold out arms from the centre post A. Then place the table top upside-down, so that the holes can be seen.

_____ Turn the table upright. It is ready to use.

_____ Attach feet D and E to centre post A, using plate Z and four screws.

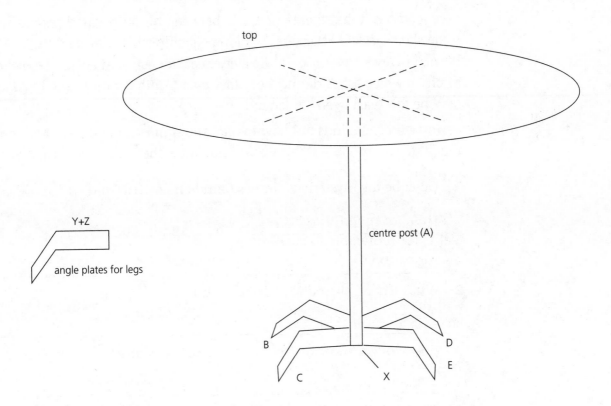

Term 4

Narrative

Read the text and answer the questions.

Island of Mystery: Easter Island

Easter Island, one of the most interesting islands in the world, is found in the South Pacific off the coast of Chile. The island, volcanic in origin, was discovered by a Dutch Admiral on Easter Sunday, 1722.

Mysterious statues of a remote and unknown origin are found on Easter Island. The statues consist of giant heads, which face inland and fringe the island's coastline. They stand on huge platforms, which slope landward. At the end of the sloping platform there is a paved area. The heads have upturned faces tilted towards the sky, and long ears.

There are 260 platforms on the island and each one was built to support between one and fifteen giant heads carved from volcanic rock.

Other mysteries to be found on the island include ancient, long, narrow boat-shaped houses flanked by stone chicken huts.

Legend has it that there was a war between the long-eared people and some short-necked attackers. The long-eared people were said to have been burned in a vast oven. Scientific evidence suggests that a vast defensive ditch, in which ashes dating from the seventeenth century have been found, may be the "vast oven" of legend.

Until someone finds out how to read the sign language inscribed round the platforms of the statues, we will not know the real truth of Easter Island.

1   Describe the mysterious statues found on Easter Island.

_____

_____

2   What legend surrounds Easter Island?

_____

3   How will we know the real truth of Easter Island?

_____

4   What is your explanation for the mysterious statues?

_____

_____

Transaction

Introducing a guest speaker

You have invited a guest speaker to come to your class. Write a speech you would make to introduce the speaker.

Include at least the following.

- Give the person's name and title.
- Give information about the person's background: occupation, any outstanding things the speaker has done.
- Give the title of the speaker's talk.
- Ask the audience to welcome the speaker.

_____

_____

_____

_____

_____

_____

_____

_____

_____

_____

_____

_____

_____

Procedure

How to fold a jacket neatly to put into a backpack

Write how you would perform the activity in no more than six steps.
Think about it before you start. Use simple sketches to help you explain
what to do.

1 _____

2 _____

_____

_____

3 _____

4 _____

_____

_____

5 _____

6 _____

_____

_____

Letter writing

1 Write a formal letter of thanks to a speaker whom you have introduced to your class. Use correct punctuation.
Use:
- a paragraph for each point
- proper punctuation in each paragraph
- formal greetings and a formal closure.

Include:
- the occasion
- the day and the month
- your thanks.

2 Address an envelope, using correct punctuation, to go with the letter. Remember to include the person's surname (family name), the number and the name of the street, the name of the suburb or town, the name of the province or territory either in full or abbreviated, the postal code and to use capital letters where required.